Woodstock Revisited

50 Far Out, Groovy, Peace-Loving, Flashback-Inducing Stories From Those Who Were There

by Susan Reynolds

Dedication

I dedicate this anthology to the 400,000-500,000 people who attended Woodstock, as well as the promoters, the performers, and all the people behind the scenes. We came together in peace and harmony and showed the world that love is possible, in the worst conditions—excessive heat, humidity, thunderstorms, and downpours, when exhausted, uncomfortable, hungry, thirsty, mud-caked, and stranded. I am grateful to you all for sharing that experience and for proving that masses of like-minded people can create a positive experience that affects the entire world. It mattered, we mattered, and it was far, far more than a huge party. That many people crammed together in lousy conditions could have turned on each other and created chaos and disaster. Instead, we endured, helped each other, and chilled. Sure, drugs were rampant, but I was there, I was drug-free the entire time, and I saw thousands and thousands just like me—ordinary kids in an extraordinary situation. So, to my brothers and sisters (literal and figurative), I express my camaraderie using the vernacular of the times—peace man!

Contents

Acknowledgments

I offer gratitude to my sister Rozanne Reynolds for letting me stay—rent-free—in her apartment that crazy summer of 1969, and to my brother Roy Reynolds who hitched up from Manorville, Pennsylvania to go to Woodstock and helped me feel safer in that impossibly huge crowd. Roy has been a musician since age fourteen, has a garage filled (literally) with at least 4,000 albums carefully stored on shelves, and spent years verifying which groups we saw at Woodstock and which ones we only thought we saw. (Blame it on the movie, which we must have watched a dozen times over the years.) I would also like to thank the late Tom Kaczmarek, who ferried us there and back and who later fathered Michele and Chris, whom we adore. I would also like to offer gratitude to my brother Jim Reynolds, who did not attend Woodstock with us, but who deserves accolades—and has always had our respect—for serving his country in Vietnam, and who also sustains a deep love for his family and music, especially the blues.

At Adams Media, I'd specifically like to thank Karen Cooper, Paula Munier, Phil Sexton, Wendy Simard, Brendan O'Neill, Matt Glazer, Beth Gissinger-Rivera, and everyone else from production to sales for their enthusiasm and support. Thank you for offering us this opportunity to record our historical accounts of that remarkable event. I also sincerely thank the contributors for taking us all on this unique journey and for chronicling an important time in our nation's history. I loved your stories and am proud to be shoulder-to-shoulder with you once again.

And finally, as always, I thank my beloved children, Brooke Ford and Brett Aved, for joining me on this incredible journey called life.

Introduction

In the summer of 1969, America seemed divided, corrupted, and on the verge of disintegration. Peace demonstrations, civil rights marches, and riots had filled our streets with thousands of disgruntled souls, each seeking to break through barriers. Thanks to the draft, we had 500,000 soldiers in Vietnam, which led to a proliferation of anti-war demonstrations at colleges and universities across the country—and in Europe. An organization called Students for a Democratic Society had staged "sit-in" demonstrations and thereby seized control of buildings on the Columbia University campus.

In 1968, two beacons of hope and inspiration, Martin Luther King and Robert F. Kennedy, had been assassinated, leaving young Americans feeling betrayed and rebellious. After King's death, race riots raged so violently in more than 100 cities, 65,000 National Guard troops were required to quell the disturbances. Later that same year, in Chicago, during the Democratic convention, police attacked and bloodied anti-war protestors.

Drugs were rampant, with Timothy Leary encouraging youthful legions to "turn on, tune in, and drop out." The National Organization for Women was encouraging young women to burn their bras and demand their equal rights. Alas, the 1967 "Summer of Love" had gone so sour that Richard Nixon won the presidential election.

Is it any wonder then that the Woodstock festival, touting three days of peace and music in 1969, became one of the most unique and legendary events in world history? Widely regarded as one of the greatest moments in popular music history, it was listed in Rolling Stone's "50 Moments That Changed the History of Rock and Roll." Because 186,000 advance tickets were sold, organizers had anticipated that approximately 200,000 people would show up, but so many came, the fences were torn down and all roads into and out of the area became log-jammed—the New York State Thruway was even closed temporarily due to extraordinary traffic.

The festival materialized amidst highly controversial military conflict abroad and unnerving racial discord at home, and became a huge counterculture party, where hippies and ordinary youth mingled to celebrate and watch some of the most prominent musical artists of the 1960s perform—Jimi Hendrix; The Who; Crosby, Stills, Nash & Young; Joe Cocker; The Band; Sly and The Family Stone; Creedence Clearwater Revival; Janis Joplin; Santana; Jefferson Airplane, and many others. Lack of seating, downpours, oozing mud, food and water shortages, and poor sanitation failed to dampen the spirits of attendees, who blended, bonded, and got along swimmingly.

Those 400,000-500,000 youth gathered at Woodstock were lauded, for three days in August 1969, as a countercultural mini-nation, the third largest "city" in New York, and the visual of a burgeoning baby boomer revolution. Minds were open, drugs were available, fantastic music filled the air, and "free love" abounded. Even today, forty years after the main event, Woodstock 1969 remains legendary throughout the world. This anthology honors the fortieth anniversary by being the first to collect stories from the perspective of those "ordinary" people who attended the three-day love fest.

While each story in Woodstock Revisited focuses on the Woodstock experience, together they illustrate America in the late sixties and how the baby boomer generation evolved. These stories go beyond tales of being caught in traffic or mired in the mud. They reflect what was going on in the minds of those hardy souls who traveled to Woodstock, and thus what was going on in our nation. It's a fascinating mix of history, humor, and passion. So come on down to Yasgur's farm and hear our tales about three days of peace and music in the hallowed fields of our youth.

Coming Around Again

By Susan Reynolds

Because my family was as divided as our country at the time (one brother had fought in Vietnam; the other threatened to move to Canada) and I was an antsy teenager, I leapt at any chance to escape the arguments at home and the sleepy town on the banks of the Allegheny River where we lived. Thus, I spent the summer of 1969 living with my sister (who was fresh out of airline school) and her three female roommates in a cramped one-bedroom apartment in Queens.

When local radio stations in New York began advertising several outdoor rock festivals, Rozanne, our brother, Roy (the conscientious objector), and I set our sights on the Woodstock festival. We had not pre-purchased tickets and had little real idea of what we would encounter.

Nevertheless, the three of us, and Rozanne's boyfriend, Tom, struck out Friday night.

Long before we approached the exit, cars had ground to a standstill and police were urging everyone to turn around and go home. Even more intrigued, we pulled our car over, slept a few hours, and then backtracked to a local grocery store and asked if there was a back way in. There was, and eventually, we squeezed the car into a tight spot and eagerly joined the cavalcade of pilgrims.

Once inside the trampled gates, Roy and I separated from Rozanne and Tom (we don't remember why or how.). For the next eighteen hours, Roy and I sat among a burgeoning group of strangers—a sea of youth. The smell of marijuana wafted through the air so thickly we experienced a contact high. Although I was afraid to accept the offered tokes, Roy gamely indulged. I was still a "good girl" who had not yet broken free of parental and societal strictures. Plus, an announcer kept spreading the word that this or that "acid is bad," and I worried that the marijuana cigarettes might have other drugs laced into the weed.

Despite this wariness, I felt oddly safe, immersed in my generation's culture, one with the swelling crowd, an amoeba in a far larger organism, symbiotic and minuscule. The music bonded us; our humanity engulfed us; our sense of global significance embodied and empowered us as a swaggering band of youthful dreamers. "The counterculture," as they called us, had a visual—400,000 yearning children, as one, portrayed credibility, voice, adrenaline, vision. Our longings for peace, for change, for brilliant futures for ourselves as individuals, and for the human race as one beat as loudly as the thundering drums onstage.

What I remember specifically is perching on an abandoned Maxwell House coffee can; sleeping curled into fetal position on a piece of shared cardboard that slid around in the oozing mud; the forcefulness of an omnipresent anti-war sentiment; the army helicopters circling overhead; and the dangerous paranoia and anger they generated. Was the government going to spy on us, threaten us, disband us, or gas us? I remember the cheers that arose when the announcer told us they were bringing us food, water, and medical supplies, and that someone on board had flashed a peace sign.

I remember the joyful, even jubilant, atmosphere that followed, crawling up a muddy hillside by grabbing outstretched hands, standing in long lines to use the foul-smelling portable toilets, being hungry, wet, tired, and thirsty. Through it all, I remember the music and how it bound us together. One after another, musicians and groups played the songs that we already loved or would grow to love. They were our anthem, our identity, and the demarcation line from that of our parents. These were our troubadours, the truth-tellers, the rebels we admired and emulated.

I remember walking through the chilled night air at 4 A.M., retracing our steps until we reached the car and crawled inside to sleep. I remember the trip home; our tongues wagging with tales; our recognition that we had all gone through something so extraordinary that going back to our everyday lives would not erase it. Our country was in turmoil, but 450,000 contemporaries came together to celebrate life, music, and joy and had the phenomenal experience of realizing that we were one. What I remember most is the sense that my generation could make a difference—that the world would soon become ours to ruin or to save.

Prior to Woodstock, I had attended peace demonstrations and often stood warily on the sidelines, watching others raise signs, make speeches, chant slogans, and taunt "the establishment," as we called them. After Woodstock, I moved more freely into the fray, even planted myself on the floor of a local university library during a "sit in," and told my mother I was spending the weekend at a friend's house when, in actuality—a short time after the Ohio National Guard murdered four students at Kent State—I piled into a Chevy Impala with seven other girls and rode to Washington, D. C., where I saw, for the first time in an up-close-and-personal way, soldiers lining the streets of Washington, their guns trained on us. Buoyed by the strength in our numbers and the memories of Woodstock, I gathered my generation's ideals to my heart and stood shoulder-to-shoulder with students shouting for an end to the Vietnam War.

I was never a hippie—not even close—unlike my sister who loved dirty, ratty jeans, I neatly pressed my bellbottoms. But I was an idealistic dreamer who went on to become a reporter, a field in which ideals served me well. Rozanne and Roy—who was a hippie briefly—became teachers, molding young souls in important ways. For years afterwards, we gleefully reminisced about Woodstock. But it wasn't until I was living in Paris in 2003 that I had another "Woodstock moment."

I had only been in Paris a few months and did not speak the language, but accompanied a Parisian friend to the anti-war demonstration leading up to the invasion of Iraq. The air was electric, the mood jovial despite the reason we had gathered. As we waited for hours for the march to begin, new arrivals by the hundred of thousands filled the street, tightening our personal space to a few inches. The lines of police multiplied, and feelings intensified until someone placed a huge speaker on the roof of his truck and blasted, We Are Family . . . and suddenly everyone sang and danced, as one, and I felt just as I had felt thirty-four years earlier, in a muddy field on Max Yasgur's farm.

To this day, memories of Woodstock make me yearn for those heady days when the youth of America took up the sword. Woodstock wasn't a dream, it happened, and like the photograph of our planet from space, it affected the way many of us viewed the world and our place in it. The phenomenon of Woodstock created waves in world consciousness, and the seemingly boundless creativity that had taken root throughout the decade blossomed. For no less than that, it's worth remembering and honoring, and perhaps more importantly, because many young people today yearn for a similarly empowering experience. Oh, if we could rise again in solidarity and strength, we could once again transform the world.

Breakfast in Bed for 400,000

By Lisa Law

At the Aspen Meadows Summer Solstice in New Mexico in 1969, Stan Goldstein, on behalf of Woodstock Ventures, Inc., asked the Hog Farm commune and the Jook Savages, a group of artists and musicians who had participated in Ken Kesey's Acid Test in Watts to handle the coordination of the campgrounds at the upcoming Woodstock Music & Art Fair. Since the Hog Farm, of which I was a member, was a large communal group, he thought we would know how to take care of masses of people, especially if they were taking drugs. We were well versed in those departments, so agreed to become caretakers and food preparers for what was expected to be about 50,000 people a day.

Our party of about eighty-five, with fifteen Indians from the Santa Fe Indian School, turned up on the assigned day at the Albuquerque International Airport to take the American Airlines jumbo jet the organizers had sent down from New York to fly us to the festival. My husband, Tom Law, and I decided to take our tipi to stay in while there, and the baggage handlers looked like Keystone Kops loading the poles into the baggage compartment. It had to have been a first.

Many reporters met us at New York's Kennedy Airport. They wanted to know if we were handling security at Woodstock. One reporter asked Wavy Gravy, our "minister of talk," what he was going to use for crowd control. He answered, "Seltzer bottles and cream pies."

From the airport, we were whisked off to White Lake in big, comfortable buses and made camp with members of our crew who had arrived earlier, having driven from New Mexico in buses loaded with supplies. Ken Kesey's bus, along with four others, came from Oregon loaded with forty Pranksters, minus Kesey himself, with his best friend Ken Babbs at the helm.

We had nine days to put together the free stage, medical tents, free food kitchen, serving booths, and information centers, and to set up the trip tents for those who, having partaken in mind-expanding drugs, needed to escape the noise, lights, people, and rain.

6

The advance crew had built a wooden dome, covered it with plastic and had set up a full kitchen inside. Max Yasgur, our host, provided us with fresh milk, yogurt, and eggs every day. Bonnie Jean Romney, Wavy Gravy's wife, was in charge of the kitchen and had gathered together odds and ends of aluminum pots and pans.

We got a flash that the concert could be much, much larger than what was projected. I traveled to New York City and spent $6,000 on food and supplies, including 1,200 pounds of bulgur wheat and rolled oats, two dozen 25-pound boxes of currants, almonds and dried apricots, 200 pounds of wheat germ, five wooden kegs of soy sauce, and five big kegs of honey, 130,000 paper plates and spoons and forks, about 50,000 paper Dixie cups, pots, pans, five huge stainless steel bowls, and thirty-five plastic garbage pails to mix large portions of muesli. I also bought 250 enameled cups for our crew and our volunteers. (There was no recycling in those days and we were into conservation.)

As Friday approached, things were looking good. The stage was almost built, but there were too many fences to be built and the turnstiles never got up. More and more people would just walk right up to a fence, lay it down and walk over it. Then they would plop themselves down on tarps, make a cushion of their sleeping bags, take off their tops to enjoy the sun, and wait for the music. There must have been 50,000 of these squatters on the main field Friday morning. The promoters told Tom and Wavy Gravy it was time to clear the fields and to start taking tickets. Wavy said, "Do you want to have a good movie or a bad movie?" The producers had a palaver and decided to make the festival free.

People just kept coming, a tidal wave of people. When the amphitheater ran out of space, communities popped up everywhere else. The free stage across the forest and down by the Hog Farm camp had its own music and audience. Some of those groups, and some of the crew, never even saw the main stage. The festival chiefs had hired off duty police to help with traffic and crowd control. They wore T-shirts that read Please Force. It was supposed to establish peaceful security. It worked.

It rained Friday night and on and off all throughout the festival. What were once beautiful grassy fields became mud bogs and slides. It would start to pour, people would stand up and just let the water rush over them. Then they would sit down again, not wanting to leave their place lest they lose it. Everyone was sharing their food with their neighbors. All the food concessions started giving their food away and the National Guard dropped supplies from planes. I would go to a neighboring farm with a truck and buy whole rows of vegetables. On Saturday morning, after Tom taught yoga off the main stage, Wavy got up and said, "What we have in mind is breakfast in bed for 400,000."

Realizing that a lot of people on the main field were not eating at all, late on Saturday we filled twenty-five of the plastic trash cans with muesli mix and served it out of Dixie cups at the side of the stage along with cups of fresh water to wash it down.

I had a Super 8 camera and about forty reels of film and was shooting everything that was happening with that and my trusty Nikon. Once a day I would hail a helicopter, say I was with the Hog Farm, and get a lift into the sky. Yeow, what a view! We had created our own city, a half a million loving, sharing freaks. I could see the traffic for miles. People were still coming. Traffic was backed up all the way to the interstate. The lake behind the stage was filled with naked bathers. Helicopters were everywhere, dropping off and picking up performers who had no other way to get into the festival.

Sleep was the furthest thing from my mind. I think I got one hour a day. I was seven months pregnant with our son, Solar. Tom and I were pretty busy multi-tasking, so Pilar, our two-year-old daughter, spent most of the time with the rest of the Hog Farm kids. On Sunday I got my first shower when the Hog Farmers rigged up a hose at the top of a ladder to be aimed down on the naked bodies below.

I know the music at Woodstock was phenomenal. They said Crosby, Stills, Nash & Young played their second gig there and that Santana wooed the crowd with master drummer Michael Shrieve backing him up. Jimi Hendrix played the National Anthem and made that guitar sing like no one else had ever done. But for me, Woodstock was the people, the masses getting along with each other, sharing, caring, doctoring, feeding. Woodstock marked the dawning of the Age of Aquarius and revealed the soul of the sixties generation awakening. The vibe that made Woodstock a household word lives on in many parts of the world. It's the force that drives us to save the planet, to bring aid to other countries, and to make things right for native cultures. The spirit of that soul, that Woodstock vibe, will endure. After all, we are all members of the same family on Turtle Island.

Lisa Law's movies, books, and still photos chronicle social and cultural changes. Flashing on the Sixties, her documentary film, has won four major awards at film festivals and been viewed on The Discovery Channel, Cinemax, and PBS. Her book by the same title is now in its fourth edition, and her newest book, Interviews with Icons, provides the complete interviews from her documentary. The Smithsonian and the Museum of New Mexico History collect her work. For more information, see www.flashingonthesixties.com.

Flashbackwards-and-Forwards

By Jeremiah Horrigan

Dec. 31, 1969

I got buttonholed at Buffalo's Main Place Mall and was asked by the "enquiring reporter" for the morning paper to name the greatest event of the 1960s.

Next day, I read the news, oh boy. The first four guys said the moon walk. The next one said the Nixon administration. I chose Woodstock. I called it a cosmic event.

An entire city got a big laugh out of that one.

Monday afternoon, Aug.18, 1969

My high school buddy Kenny is at the wheel of his big-ass Galaxie 500. I and another friend named Kester man the eight-track up front while the two young women who had chastely accompanied us on the trip from Buffalo to Bethel sit primly in the back seat. The Galaxie has a monster V-8 and Kenny likes to move. We are, as the song says, goin' home.

Suddenly, a flashing cherry top in the rearview. A siren.

A speed trap.

Kenny's pissed, but innocent of the real problem. He doesn't know, as I do, that Kester's holding a lid of grass. Neither of us feels the need to confess just now.

Historical note: People did serious prison time in 1969 for possession of grass. And not just the people who were holding.

The state trooper struts over to Kenny's window and informs him he's been doing 90 in a 60. The trooper takes Kenny's license, sticks his head in the window, and casts his steely gaze across us mud-spattered refugees.

The air is redolent of cow.

Kenny, I, and Eileen are three about-to-be college sophomores, still as straight looking as our high school graduation portraits. Babe, the sister of a friend, is in high school and looks even more innocent, if not straighter. Kester is the only guy with long hair we know.

I'm dizzy with fear and a newfound love for all humanity. The silence is killing me.

"You guys did a great job back at the festival, officer."

The trooper freezes, stares at me. He doesn't seem eager to claim credit. Kenny looks ready to throttle me.

The trooper returns to his cruiser and takes a very long time running Kenny's license. We wait. The trooper returns. Without a word, he bends over and peers in at us again. Stands back up. Rips a ticket from his book. Then he was gone. No questions. No vehicle search. No arrests. Without so much as a "Hi Ho, Silver," the most understanding state trooper in all of New York state has patched out in a cloud of dust.

It's only hours since Woodstock ended, and already the forces of peace and love have won the day.

Earlier that same morning . . .

The sun is coming up over the all-but-deserted field in front of the stage. I'm spaced, having eaten only a couple of stuffed olives and some watermelon since our arrival.

The field looks like the bottom of a lake that's just been drained—busted furniture, pieces of lumber, sleeping bags, and blankets all plopped in ankle-deep, super-natural-smelling muck. I feel planted to the spot, afraid I'll lose my sneakers if I move.

Jimi Hendrix is onstage, looking extremely cool. He's playing a song that's strangely familiar but whose title escapes me. Hendrix hardly seems to be moving as he wrings these fantastic sounds from his guitar. It's some kind of sonic attack, all vibrato and wah-wah and feedback.

Then it hits me like a mortar shell: America the Beautiful. He's playing America the Beautiful!

I think.

I look around and see a skinny guy in what looks like a toga planted in the nearby muck.

"He's playing America the Beautiful!" I scream.

"The Star-Spangled Banner," he shouts. "It's the fucking Star-Spangled Banner!"

"Right! Right! Holy Shit!"

I stand as if struck by lightning, amazed, and listen to Jimi Hendrix play the fucking Star-Spangled Banner. It's beautiful.

Sometime Sunday . . .

Who invited Sha-Na-Na to the party?

Saturday afternoon

I score some dope. Kester is the only guy in our entourage who smokes, and I'd lost track of him hours before. I'm suddenly paranoid. I stand surrounded by half a million hippies—or, in my case, hippie wannabes—and I'm scared of getting busted for dope.

So I do the obvious thing. I walk about three miles back to where we'd pitched a little pup tent and I climb inside, zipping and snapping the flap closed behind me. I roll an inept joint.

But paranoia strikes deep. Into my tent it does creep. I hear voices and panic, ripping the joint up, spreading the dope like flaming fertilizer on the tent floor, flapping my arms at the bit of incriminating smoke I'd generated. Then I start all over again as soon as things quiet down.

Confession: I was the only guy at Woodstock to get stoned by hyperventilating in a pup tent.

Friday Afternoon

We arrive. Richie Havens, the opening act, cries for freedom. But problems abound. Kenny and Kester haven't bought advance tickets. We ditch the car, pitch our tent, and go looking.

Magic happens. We find a guy wearing a red bandana and standing in front of a knocked-down snow fence. He offers to sell us tickets for $20. "Far out," I say.

Cackling with delight at our big score, we make the buy and go looking for the ticket-taker.

Forty years later

Kenny's license was suspended for three months following the trip home. We're still best friends. Kester got married and disappeared from my life. Likewise the girls.

Kenny and I got mixed up, two years after Woodstock, in separate draft board rip-offs. I got busted, but didn't do time. He was the wheelman in a different action and didn't get caught. He's now an executive in a big insurance company, and I'm now a newspaper reporter.

And what did this "cosmic event" have to do with anything? Well, on New Year's Day, 1970, I gave the city of Buffalo something to laugh about. But who, I ask you, has had the last laugh?

Jeremiah Horrigan is a newspaper reporter for the (Middletown, New York) Times Herald-Record. Over the years, his work has appeared in Sports Illustrated, The New York Times, The Miami Herald, and Negligent Mother Magazine. He has yet to nail The New Yorker's caption contest, but he will not be denied. Having decided that what the world needs now is a new blog, he and his son Grady are developing www.good-humor-men.blogspot.com, a blog devoted to grown-up humor.

The Haze Wasn't Purple

By Louis Mello

I know there was a road. Cars backed up for miles, and what had once been two lanes was transformed into a one way fast-lane opening onto a paradise of music and freedom that my fourteen-year-old mind vividly, and in splashing Technicolor®, imagined, as though reflected on the big screen through the lens of Kubrick's celebrated descent on Jupiter—the bringer of jollity. Little did we travelers imagine that a bend of history was about to occur.

After feverishly wrangling fifteen dollars from my hard-working father—whose suspicions of, as he bluntly stated, "three days of pot, peace, and pussy" turned out to be very well-founded—I kicked in with my own hefty savings, three crumpled one dollar bills, to make up the eighteen needed for the full advance-ticket trifecta. I thought I was headed to a great concert, not to the crepuscule of our, occasionally childish and ostensibly malcontented counter-culture. The tickets turned out to be as useful as the food we hadn't packed. But we did have a canteen brimming with Canadian Club spiked H2O.

My father offered to drive Reb and me the forty some-odd miles from our upstate vacation house to Bethel. Reb—short for rebel, as in the Confederate Army, which was the appellation preferred by my friend Phillip Horowitz— wasn't originally supposed to go with me. My comrade of all hours, Lloyd, was slated to be in that car. For reasons that now escape memory, he could not make the trip.

Patience was not one of the elder Mello's virtues . . . my father quickly realized that these cars were not going to move anywhere anytime in the next three days. He laughingly told us we were on our own. "No big deal, we are no more than a mere fifteen miles from the site," he said. It was, after all, our time, and we could get a ride with someone else.

We did. A young, blonde hippie couple invited us into their Beetle convertible, which was packed tightly with an assortment of musical instruments. They didn't seem to mind two acne-ridden, greasy-haired kids from Brooklyn, who were now indulging wantonly in Reb's stolen-whisky laced canteen, while adoring the tie-dyed upholstery of their car.

So, amid the guitar cases and the paper bags, we sat, and drank and talked about what lay ahead.

"The Airplane, man . . . "

"No, no . . . Alvin Lee . . . Hendrix . . ."

And we filled the next five hours with booze, some Mary Jane, courtesy of our hosts, and banter about music, politics, and drugs. I guess they both felt we were too young to talk about sex.

When we got out of the car, the fences were already down. Shouts were heard everywhere:

"Now it's a free concert, man . . . "

"We've liberated the grounds!"

I stared emptily at the tickets in my hand. I thought of all the other good uses those eighteen dollars might have had. Thus, we trampled the green pastures of Max Yasgur's farm, home to the Woodstock Music & Art Fair.

The asphyxiating August heat and humidity were not even an afterthought. I didn't see Reb again until the morning of our exodus; we missed Hendrix as he famously twisted and bowed and contorted The Star Spangled Banner.

I wish I could tell you, kind reader, that I was among those who chanted for rain; that I went skinny dipping in the lake (that body of water that I only glimpsed in the movie, ten years after—pun intended), sliding along the mud tracks, dancing in an acid induced frenzy to the music of my generation (pun also intended). But that would not be true. I did none of those things. In fact, when I saw the film I wondered if it was indeed the same concert.

The following three days progressed in the manner of an opium-laden dream. I remember hearing music, some of which sounded like radio static. Some of it was as clear as Poe's The Bells. Some of it I knew, some of it sounded as if it had originated on a distant planet, in a faraway galaxy. There was rain, as I sat under an impromptu tent and smoked something.

I recollect a farm boy type with long straggling hair who cheerily informed me that he had "a good ol' case of the American runs . . . " He then proceeded to offer me a pipe, the contents of which remain a mystery to this day.

In the middle of a dense thunderstorm I encountered a platinum-haired, alabaster-skinned, nubile nymph who told me in a thundering voice that I had to head over to the back woods . . . there would be food there I would also be able to hang out with the Grateful Dead.

"Jerry is there," she said, in a knowing tone.

I was a staunch Dylan freak, and the Dead were banda non grata in my neck of the woods. This made me ponder, probably the only rational sequence of ideas to cross my mind for the entire three-day span: Why wasn't Dylan there?

Still, the wraith, as she has only been known in the recondite recesses of my faulty memory, led me by the hand to a clearing. Picnic tables were scattered with paper plates and cups; the ground was virtually carpeted in plastic utensils. There were several people behind a makeshift table dishing out an ocher soup-like substance from a huge vat. That was my first and only meal. I didn't see Jerry, or anyone else resurrected from the Dead.

The next thing I remember was waking up on a rock-hard church pew, somewhere in the vicinity of Monticello, waiting for a good soul to offer a ride back to the city. This came in the form of an insurance salesman from New Paltz who was just passing through, but had heard tell of the concert.

Reb appeared along the side of the road, mysteriously as fresh and well scrubbed as the day we had left. We never talked about our apparently disparate experiences, I guess in much the same way Army buddies don't like to reminisce.

Our savior left us in the Bronx, from where we headed back to Brooklyn, so much the wiser for having survived, first hand, the true meaning of the word haze.

Louis Mello, a native New Yorker, has worked as mathematician and writer. He has lived both in the United States and in Brazil and has written poetry and fiction. His work was included in a Brazilian anthology of young poets. Recent short stories have appeared in the journals ProgressChrome and Conte Online.

A Republican Hippie on Max Yasgur's Farm
By John M. DeVoe

It was our last high school summer. My friends hitched to White Lake from our hometown of Brookville, a small town north of Pittsburgh. I scored a last-minute ride with Fred, an AM rock DJ I knew. Soon after Fred and I arrived, we spied Rich, Ken, and Jim walking up through the woods. After maneuvering through a seething tangle of people and cars, we had somehow managed to park about twenty yards from my friends' newly constructed lean-to.

Day one was all folk. Not my thing, so I roamed the turf alone, as was my way. Deep in the woods, two ancient and worn paths crossed: High Way and Groovy Way. Both were lit with miniature Christmas lights and lined with makeshift stalls and shanties, from which hippie merchants sold tie-dyed T-shirts, incense, pottery, leather goods, and head supplies. I had never smoked dope, but I bought a brass belt buckle with a removable hash pipe—just in case.

As night fell, I gathered deadfall and helped some West Coast freaks build a bonfire. We passed a joint and talked music and politics. The thought of tripping scared the shit out of me, but I figured I had to make my hippie bones sometime so I accepted and imbibed mescaline and pretty much hated every minute of it. I experienced zero spiritual enlightenment, zero sense of oneness with the universe, not even any lurid visions. Random apocalyptic thoughts eventually compelled me to seek the Hog Farm's freakout tent.

A woman handed me a cup of hot tea, talked to me calmly, put her arm around me, and walked me around a little. Even though she was at least thirty—ancient in those days, and, according to our gurus, untrustworthy—I put the moves on her. She laughed and said, "If you're sane enough to be horny, you'll be OK. Get out of here."

I found a giant communal teepee full of sleeping people, crawled inside, and spent a fitful night, half-dozing as the mescaline continued to kick my ass. When I opened my eyes, I saw walls printed with a trippy Aztec design, but when I asked someone about this, he laughed and said, "No, man, it's a fuckin' standard green tent."

Turned out, the tent was about a five-minute walk from our campsite, where I found Jim, Ken, and Rich trying to rebuild the lean-to after the rains had reduced it to a pile of sticks and leaves.

"Where the fuck were you?" Ken asked.

"I did some mesc and wandered around like a zombie all night," I told him.

"You still trippin'? You look like fuck-all." Rich said.

"Thanks. A little, I guess. It sucks."

"Hang on," Ken said, and gave me a handful of pills.

"What are these?" I asked.

"Geritol. I did some acid and started to freak, so some guy gave me half a bottle of Geritol."

I swallowed a bunch and crashed like a sack of brass. Soon after, reality roared back, and I was damn glad to see it.

We stashed our stuff, what there was of it, and headed to the concert. We found our way to a spot about thirty feet from the stage. And then, some naked guy with bushy hair and a scraggly beard climbed a sound tower and started shaking it with both hands. We were afraid it would collapse, or that the guy would start pissing on our heads. Neither happened. Late in the day, National Guard helicopters flew over dropping baloney sandwiches and Best Cola.

Sha Na Na's singer, Bowser, I think, started their set by proclaiming, "I got one thing to tell you fuckin' hippies: Rock and roll is here to stay! " Creedence was better than I expected, but The Dead sucked. Badly. When they had sound problems, Bob Weir tried to calm the booing crowd with a little standup. He was not Catskills material.

Much later, Abbie Hoffman jumped onstage with The Who, grabbed the mike, and said some bullshit like: "You people listen to this bullshit while John Sinclair rots in prison for two lousy joints!" Pete Townshend slammed him in the face with the headstock of his SG, knocking him back into the crowd. Later, Pete pitched his guitar offstage, and I missed it by about a foot.

When we finally headed back and discovered the lean-to had become a hopeless ruin, we headed to Fred's car. I woke up to the thud of copter blades and blinding light. An Army helicopter hovered over the entrance to the grounds, lighting the field with its night sun.

The rain had finally stopped, but people leaving the stage area were covered in mud. Lines of people filed back to their cars or campgrounds, some falling or skidding, some calling out to missing friends. A dignified black man in a silk dashiki swung a flashlight in a wide arc. "Plasma?" he called repeatedly, giving us no clue whether he was buying or selling. One guy carried a double handful of leftover acid he was offering at closeout prices. "Acid!" he chanted "Four hits for a buck!" When he slipped in the mud, spilling his precious dope into the writhing slime underfoot, a crowd swarmed around him, scooping up and literally eating the mud.

Caught up in the madness, I screamed my angst-ridden teenage horniness to the sky. "I want to ball someone now!"

"Fuck you!" Rich said.

"Fuck who?" I asked.

And Jim answered with the phrase that captured the manitou of White Lake, of our youth and our tribe, of the sixties as we lived them. It was our shout out to high school, to draft boards, to The Church, to the government—to all authority, in all its grim gray manifestations. It was love and hate, fear and hope, rage and joy—and defiance. And for me, those two words informed my weltanschauung from that day forward:

"Fuck they !"

By the time we got home, Woodstock had become a phenomenon, damned by preachers and politicians, hailed by the media. Sociologists studied it, pundits debated it, and marketers hyped, re-hyped, and then hyped it some more. When Joni Mitchell (who was not there) later sang about us as children of God on their way to Paradise, we laughed our asses off. The lean-to showed up in 60 Minutes photo-montage. A few crowd photos in Crawdaddy showed us near the stage, and when Sears brought out a matching shirt and bellbottom set with a two-tone print of the crowd, we festooned the ass of the pants. The world remembers Woodstock, but for us, Woodstock was a place that vanished. We headed for Woodstock and came back from White Lake. None of us ever called it anything else.

John DeVoe lives in Texas with his wife, Nancy, and a multitude of happy cats and dogs. He has looked for oil, practiced law, and written code.

Nothing Ventured

by Alan Kolman

Hard to believe that Woodstock was nearly forty years ago—sorry, Bob, but I really don't feel so much younger now.

I was lucky enough to have actually worked for Woodstock Ventures Inc. The offices at 47 E. 57th St. in the months leading up to the festival were a bit like a giant, jumbled psychedelic bee hive: lots of seemingly chaotic movement, buzzing, and frantic running around, but somehow work did get done. As one of the drones—my job involved ticket sales—I had a front row seat for what became one of the defining moments for my generation.

My friend Keith O'Connor got me the job—we had worked together in the Fillmore East box office—and the timing couldn't have been better. I had just been thrown out of pots and pans college after my first day and was stone cold broke. My older brother, Larry, was fighting in Vietnam, and I was trying my best not to follow him over there.

After a couple of weeks, I was able to get my friend John a job as well, and we had a blast. Everybody's freak flag was flying at full mast, the suite of offices rocked all day long. We felt like cosmic midwives giving birth to the next generation—everyone was a fuckin' star, man. The holy hippie trinity of sex, drugs, and rock n' roll was the order of the day, and we were all getting ordained.

Except maybe John Roberts, the man who had the money that made it all possible. He would show up around noon, looking like he'd just stepped off a big sailboat and taken a wrong turn. Like the rest of the bigs, he didn't have a clue, but was determined to at least look business-like. Michael Lang would sweep in and out like a chunky Roger Daltry; Artie Kornfeld kinda stumbled around with a Gomer smile most of the time; Joel Rosenman was a quiet presence; but John was serious as hell. Negotiations for venue and acts, rumors, and white powder drifted around everyone like dust motes.

The Wednesday before the festival began, many of us went up to Monticello, where most of a motel had been rented for staff. That first night, our room—John (not Roberts) and I shared one with our girlfriends—turned into some surreal Fellini movie. There had to have been at least fifty freaks in there, passing doobies, pipes and a mirror heaped with coke around for hours. After a while, we were all anesthetized enough for major surgery, and folks began to drift out the door to other parties and dimensions. By the time the four of us were alone in the room, my memory becomes as hazy as the air, my recollections a fractured kaleidoscope of images and music.

Friday we drove to the festival grounds in my old crapped out Ford Anglia. As we inched past throngs of people up the dirt road behind the stage, which was still feverishly under construction, my radiator overheated and boiled over. Water was in short supply, but we discovered that apple cider worked real well as a coolant, too.

We finally reached a small wooden construction trailer and began selling tickets. Less than a hundred feet away, the temporary fence was under assault, and finally gave way. We kept on selling tickets to the stoned out and bewildered for hours, until the announcement that it was now a free festival blasted out. By this time the only sane way in and out was helicopter, but somehow John wound up with a huge bag of cash from ticket sales, and was able to navigate his Honda 450 through the mess and deliver it to the appropriate people. Probably should have just kept it to sleep on.

Once we stopped selling tickets, we set up housekeeping in the trailer— which was great until we were evicted and it became a first aid station. When the rain began, it seemed like a perfect opportunity to grab a shower, so I got wet, went inside to soap myself head to toe and leaped back out just as the rain stopped. With soap drying all over my body, I trundled down to the pond and joined all the other naked people having some good clean fun. There was nothing sexual about it—we really were Mother Nature's children that weekend. The music, as cosmic as it was, seemed secondary to the feeling of infinite possibilities we all carried away from the event—we believed real, substantive change was just around the corner. Unfortunately, what we perceived as the birth of the Aquarian Age, was, in retrospect, more like a giant Irish wake.

When we got home, seeing the media coverage somehow made it all more real, and not just the dream of half a million opium eaters. Music is still an integral part of my life, but I'm afraid that feeling of optimism has been replaced by a sense of futility. The Woodstock generation, once we doffed our tie-dyed costumes, seems just like any other group of self-absorbed people. I guess The Who said it best: "Meet the new boss, same as the old boss."

Alan Kolman has been a stonemason, draft horse farmer, electrician, and computer technician over the intervening years, and resides outside Asheville, North Carolina. No writing credits to speak of, but a trunk full of unpublished books and movie scripts is still gathering dust somewhere. He and his then-girlfriend, Robbie, are celebrating their thirty-eighth wedding anniversary this August.

A Day in the Country

By Colleen Plimpton

An armload of biology books teetered as I bent to examine the
Newsweek magazine lying on the coffee table in our shabby student
apartment. It was late August in the long-ago summer of 1969 and I, a
college junior, was dutifully off to the library.

But the magazine's Woodstock story caught my eye, and I felt compelled
to read the article—immediately. My boyfriend, Bobby, and I were
freshly returned from the melody and mess of that weekend in upstate
New York. Yasgur farm mud still stained our bathroom floor; the music
of Santana and Joan Baez still rang in our ears, and I couldn't help but
wonder how well a mainstream periodical would represent what I already
knew to be a seminal three days in Bethel, New York.

The photo on the lower left-hand side of the second page stopped me
cold.

It couldn't be. It couldn't be.

But it was.

Out of the approximately half a million young people at the Woodstock
Music & Art Fair, a Newsweek photographer had chosen Bobby
Grohulski and me to represent a truth about Woodstock.

There we were, in all our bedraggled glory, Bobby in his scarlet plastic
cape, striding across the hilltop, and me—the only hippie at Woodstock
with an umbrella—trudging along behind him, carrying our satchel and
our sandals. We were so wet, the satchel so obviously empty, that the
photo had to have been taken on Sunday, as we, scruffy, smelly, and
exhausted, were leaving Woodstock Nation. We had had enough.

Several weeks earlier Bobby had decided to attend the festival. Not being
much into music, I was a reluctant sell until I heard where it was to be
held—my beloved upstate New York. My daydreams about life after
college had begun to involve finding a rural commune and living off the
land. This would be practice.

We bought our tickets, quit our summer jobs early, and shopped the local
Army-Navy store for what we naively believed existed—a waterproof

sleeping bag. We stuffed some canned goods in an old valise, and started hitching out of the Bronx midday Friday.

Ten miles from the site, the burgeoning slipstream of young humankind was our first clue that we were into something momentous. We jammed the road as we slogged west, sandwiched between rows of open-mouthed townsfolk standing in their front lawns, watching. They offered cups of water, handfuls of shredded lettuce, smiles.

We arrived at dusk, in time to hear Melanie. Humanity littered the ground, the food kiosks were abandoned, there were no camping spots to be had, and we didn't need our tickets to enter. The night was August-hot, the cicadas hummed during music breaks. We dropped onto a patch of open space and stretched out.

Immersed that first night in the sea of people, I figured there had to be significance in the music. Otherwise, what was everybody doing there? But I couldn't quite grasp the meaning, couldn't personalize it, hard as I pondered through the weekend's haze of ganja and acid and beer. It had a whiff of "do your own thing," but what did that represent for me?

Nevertheless, most of Friday night and Saturday were marvelous—despite the smell of mud and unwashed bodies, despite the impossible lines for portable potties, and the lack of shelter. We swayed to the music. We shared joy, joints, and food with our neighbors on the hill.

The loudspeaker informed us what drugs to avoid, how many babies had been born, and what The New York Times thought of us.

I gazed around in wonder at the smacked-flat slope that had been a farmer's field a week earlier. One side had devolved into a mudslide, down which whooping, happy people slithered, uninhibited. The marshy farm pond adjacent to the festival site was alive with swimmers, clothed and unclothed, laughing, bathing, playing toss-the-kid, or just hanging out.

It had rained Friday night. Then it rained some more Saturday, complete this time with thunder and lightning. Bobby and I huddled together in our soggy sleeping bag. Some attendees left; we were able to scoot down the hill nearer to the stage. By Sunday afternoon enough people had departed that we were close enough to see the stars on Joe Cocker's boots.

Then it really rained, and it was the last straw. Bobby hoisted our matted sleeping bag on his shoulder; I followed, and up the hill we trudged. For us, it was over.

Somewhere along the way an unseen Newsweek photographer snapped our picture.

Every so often I come across that photograph, and I'm awash in memories. Thus, I had to see the new museum that stands sentinel by the Woodstock site, commemorating both the sixties and the festival. A copse of trees opens onto the whole of the farmer's field that was Woodstock's amphitheater. I stood at that overlook and could not believe how many years had passed. Did I realize then how much my generation would revolutionize society? And did I ever really think I was going to live off the land?

I long ago misplaced Bobby Grohulski, the love of my young life. I never settled into a commune. My subsequent career had nothing to do with upstate New York, or nature. Instead, I was cubicled, meetinged, and memoed for thirty years.

But standing on that site with the mid-August sun on my middle-aged shoulders, I realized something. For the past four years, since I retired from my job, the magazines on my coffee table are more likely to be The Mother Earth News or Horticulture than Fortune. I no longer attend meetings around conference tables, nor do I send annual reports. The books I tote now concern native plants and composting.

I'm a professional gardener, and I make my living off the land.

I'd finally heard the message behind the music.

Colleen Plimpton is a gardener and a writer, whose work can be seen both in her Connecticut yard and in such publications as People, Places & Plants, The Litchfield Review, and GreenPrints. When not at the computer or the compost pile, she's busy keeping track of her three children, who reside in Beijing, China; Florida; and Bethel, Connecticut.

High Flying Bird

By Michele Kadison

That summer of 1969, my mom and dad had agreed to let me stay in a cabin behind my friend Suzi's parents' house. They had confidence in me and felt it would be a lovely way for me to spend the summer, with the beach nearby, along with a group of my friends that they knew well. My friends and I all found jobs at a candle factory in Wellfleet, just south of Provincetown on Cape Cod.

We were young and sexy girls—who adorned ourselves with love beads, headbands, wild hair, and tie-dye clothing—working in an overheated and impossibly Dickensian candle factory, where managers fined us for sitting down during a shift. We didn't mind. We fortified ourselves by slipping into the bathroom to steal tokes on a communal joint. We always had a laugh, and, besides, the guys we worked with were so damn cute.

When we heard about a huge music festival in Woodstock, we immediately sensed it would be the only place to be on the planet that summer. Determined to hitch, we paired off, and I ended up with Jimmy, a gorgeous Robert Plant look-alike. I knew we'd be safe and so I fed my parents a story about where I would be for the weekend.

In those days, hitching was a breeze. You held your thumb out, flashed the peace sign, and someone who looked like you would stop, invite you to climb in, immediately pass you a pipe, and drive you as far as they could. The weather was silky warm, the radio played fabulous music, and joints were steadily passed back and forth, passenger-to-passenger, car-to-car. Occasionally, Jimmy and I made out in the back seat because, well, that's the way it went in those days. Soon after, we'd be on the road again, me in my mini-skirt, clogs, Indian blouse, and long hair, standing in front to attract motorists. We hitched through the night and the bulk of the morning until we arrived at Yasgur's farm.

Golden light lit the scene as we walked amidst the swelling tribe of beautiful people that had also made their way to Woodstock. We paused here and there along a wide path to dip into the honey pot offered by hippies peddling everything from pot to hash to uppers and downers to mescaline to peyote—and more. Donning additional beads and feathers, we felt awash in this love fest far, far away from the madding crowd of the known straight world. We filled whatever we were carrying with "magic" and headed towards the concert site.

The image was breathtaking There we stood, on a communal blanket that seemed to stretch for acres, in a world populated by our own beautiful people, smiling, just beginning to take off on the wild journey that would become a blur of drugs and bliss—because we had come together as one.

A massive hedonistic blur of sound came next. I remember Richie Havens, dressed all in white, as if he were the high priest of welcome, singing for ages. And Country Joe and the Fish bringing us to our rebel feet, where we chanted while passing endless bottles of wine back and forth, feeling as if we were at the beginning of a new and as yet unformed world, led by this California wildman at the microphone. The good vibes and the night seemed to expand, and I remember balancing on Jimmy's shoulders as we swayed to the Incredible String Band and later madly dancing in a circle as Sly & the Family Stone brought us to our feet. And then feeling lured down into my spiritual center by Ravi Shankar's music—just before the rain began.

At first the rain was a feather kiss, cooling us and subtly bringing us back to earth; but soon the rhythm became a pounding, teeming, elemental force that had us scampering and sliding through the mud to find shelter.

Somehow Jimmy and I ended up alone in the back of an empty cabbage truck, the water beating down on the metal roof, drowning out everything around us. Later, we ran through the woods, arriving at our campsite out of breath and soaked to the bone, where we stripped off our clothing and jumped into our miraculously dry sleeping bag, shivering and laughing, as high as kites. This coupling led to my very first dose of that hallowed, sanctified combination of sex, drugs, and rock 'n roll.

We emerged the next morning and began our search, in drizzling rain, to find food and a place to dry our bones. We slogged through the mud to the main grounds where we ate soggy vegetable-filled chapattis and heard about all the drama we had missed. Someone had been run over by a tractor. Hundreds of people had been tripping on bad acid and were being treated in the aptly named freakout tent. No one was to pop anything that looked purple. Or orange. Or brown. Soon after, we smoked a joint and settled in to watch Canned Heat, Santana, etc. al. Again, wine and joints, and even kisses between strangers, flowed. The higher we got, the less we noticed the rain, or the fact we were again drenched through and through.

On Sunday, Jimmy and I wandered around aimlessly, danced in puddles, rolled in the grass, hung out with our new best friends. At one point, we became separated, and I ended up weaving flowers into crowns with a bunch of girls I didn't know. A beautiful black man wearing paisley pants and a leather vest circled us, his energy so bright he seemed angelic, an apparition who laughed and flirted and was so sexy and so very high, kissing each one of us as if we were his girlfriend. His aura brought us into the epicenter of his magnetic sexuality and it wasn't until later that I realized that it was Jimi Hendrix, wandering about unleashed.

Amazingly, my Jimmy found me in time for us to spend that night at least eight miles high, sleeping under ancient, towering oak trees while music trailed through the night. I remember hearing the wail of Johnny Winter, and then much later, Hendrix, whose shrieking reverb of guitars cut through the forest and into our sleep, waking us in amazement. As we lay there, under the dark foliage, listening, I remember wondering am I here, or am dreaming? In retrospect, the whole event was a dream . . . but my young, high-flying-bird self was also very much there.

Michele Kadison has had a long career as a dancer, teacher, and choreographer. Originally from New York, she lives in Buenos Aires, where she teaches contemporary jazz, writes, and directs her theater-dance company, La Semilla.

Five Days of Peace & Music

By Sandy McKnight

I was sixteen that summer, and had just been kicked out of prestigious Brooklyn Technical High School for my subversive political activities (I ran for student body president as a write-in candidate on the "Pot Party" ticket). I had a job in a Brooklyn shoe store, and I was subletting a fifth-story walkup on East 6th Street between 1st and 2nd Avenue in the East Village.

In front of the Fillmore East, down the block, I learned about the upcoming festival and determined I'd get there somehow. I'd been in Chicago the summer before for the police riot at the Democratic convention. A music and art festival promised to be more fun and less dangerous.

By the week of the festival, I had a plan. I would quit my job and take a bus to Monticello, which was within easy hitching distance of Bethel, the newly announced site.

That Wednesday, I "packed" a change of clothes and a bottle of cologne in a pillowcase, and set out for the Port Authority Bus Terminal.

Back in Brooklyn, my parents, who were in their late thirties, were also heading out for the festival. Recently converted to the counterculture, they couldn't wait to see Richie Havens, Joan Baez, and Tim Hardin. Of course, unlike their son, they arranged to arrive by car, bought tickets, and showed up on Friday, the day the show began.

But I knew it was going to be more than a concert, that it would be a gathering of the tribes. My plan was to arrive early, learn the lay of the land, meet some fellow hippies, and camp out in the country. The music was optional.

I arrived at the site early Wednesday evening and soon found a spot on a hill that overlooked the rear of the stage. Workers frantically labored, constructing the towers and cover for the large stage. A few hundred people were there, and as the night went on, more cars drove onto the site, many filled with excited and blissful fellow hippies. It was easy to make casual acquaintances in those days, and so I did. People passed around bottles of wine, of which I partook, somehow avoiding getting "dosed."

By Thursday, the cars arrived in a constant stream. People hitched rides on hoods, trunks, and roofs of passing cars. The hill I had staked out the night before filled up with tents, as did the area in front of the still-unfinished stage—and the concert that was still twenty-four hours away.

I remember walking into the little town of Bethel and buying a sandwich from a local. The vibe was so festive everywhere, even among the local residents, who had never seen anything like us before. The lack of commerciality was astounding.

By Friday, I knew all the back roads and could hitch my way anywhere I wanted to go. When the nearby towns ran out of food on Saturday, I hitched to Jeffersonville, about twenty miles away, and grabbed a bite. I ate at Woolworth's, then picked up a ride heading back on Route 17B, and guided my host right to a prime spot in the middle of the site. By this point, most people had to walk miles to get there.

I never saw my parents, but later learned they left Friday night after the folkies played. Since it was already a crazy scene, I couldn't blame them.

On Saturday, I met Dorothy, a nineteen-year-old girl from Cape May, New Jersey. Later, we shared a sleeping bag, and made love while The Who played Tommy as the sun rose.

During the legendary rainstorm, I ducked into an open Volkswagen Bug and sat it out. Not everyone frolicked in the mud.

A friend of mine from the Lower East Side arrived and set up camp on my hill. It was David Peel, the street musician who later recorded with John Lennon. He and his motley crew of street hippies set up an impromptu concert right off the road. I picked up a tambourine and played as he sang, "I like marijuana, you like marijuana, we like marijuana too." A large crowd gathered to join in this homemade festival.

Wow, I thought, I can say "I played at Woodstock."

All weekend, I saw the backs of the greatest music artists of the time from my perch on that hill.

By late—very late—Sunday night, only one act hadn't yet performed, and I considered Hendrix the most important artist of the weekend—the symbol of how music, and the world, had changed. The few thousand hardy souls who stayed until the sun began to rise that Monday morning were prepared for the pinnacle. We were ready to be "experienced."

Finally, as day broke, Jimi finally took the stage. I wandered onto the mud pit where the crowd once sat and which was now littered with the remains of half a million blankets, rain slickers, and programs. A few thousand hardy souls watched and listened to a legendary performance that had an odd flavor of sadness to it. We knew, as we listened, that it was over. We'd made history and "come together" but we also understood that it could never happen again. Soon there'd be Altamont and Kent State and Watergate and disco. Jimi and Janis and Jim would all die shortly thereafter, as if they knew it was all over too.

But I also felt joy that misty Monday morning. I knew I'd experienced something extraordinary and unique. I was dirty, exhausted, and hadn't eaten since Woolworth's on Saturday, but I had shared a utopia with my brothers and sisters for a brief moment in time. As the stragglers tramped down the road, I asked someone for a ride. He was going to Westchester, which was close enough. I stopped at my aunt's house in Hastings-on-Hudson, where the local kids treated me like some kind of a hero for having been there. I just wanted a shower.

Soon, I moved back to Brooklyn with my folks. The revolution was over.

Sandy McKnight became a musician, songwriter, and producer. He now writes for television, and performs his music in concert venues. His latest CD, Wise Up! is credited to his "virtual" band, The Ragamuffins of Love, and their leader, Effington (Eff) Dupp. Sandy lives in upstate New York, where he runs a not-for-profit performing arts organization

A Neurotic Child of God

By Michele Hax

There were some things I knew back in 1969. A short list of the things that seemed significant, and indicative of the times:

1....Boys had a vested interest in protesting the Vietnam War.

2....I had a vested interest in boys.

3....Tear gas did more than its name implies; it caused nausea as well.

4....I could wear any top I wanted without a bra.

5....With my long and thick hair, floppy hats, and loads of jewelry, I looked a lot like Janis Joplin.

6....Abortions were illegal. (Roe v. Wade legalized (some) abortions in 1973.)

7....Griswold v. Connecticut had legalized birth control (the Pill!) for married couples, and even though single girls wouldn't win the same legal permission until 1972, some managed to find their own pipeline.

8....My dates took me to see most of the era's great bands.

a....No one was better than Mick Jagger when he teased the crowd by waving his jacket as if he was winding up for a lob into the sixth row of the Civic Center (not impossible).

b....Sitting in the second row seats for the Doors at the Lyric, and gazing up at Jim Morrison propped on a microphone dangling dangerously close to the audience while the band played Light My Fire . . . for an hour: fabulous.

c....Lightning and thunder crashing all around the outside stage while Pink Floyd played The Dark Side of the Moon . . . for an hour: mind-blowing.

9....Pretty much all the liquids at rock concerts or in park gatherings were laced with acid.

10....I was going to Woodstock.

I wasn't completely cognizant of any big happening called Woodstock when my "boyfriend" asked me to go. I agreed to go with the eagerness and enthusiasm one might expect from someone who loved rock concerts and one who was completely oblivious of the logistics. Little did I realize at the time the historical significance of Woodstock—and its cache among my sociology students that dated me, with impunity.

Thus, in a two-seat MG largely containing a tiny cooler loaded with two steaks (seriously) thrown on top of ice, we headed toward upstate New York. Woodstock. Unlike my other rock concert dates, this one did not go well.

Initially, inching towards Woodstock was a fantastical experience. People ditched their cars, hoisted their backpacks on their shoulders and walked long distances down a dusty dirt road, looking ecstatic. VW buses—some brightly colored and hand-painted with groovy peace signs or flowers—sat along the edges of the woodsy roadside, where hippies perched blissfully on their roofs flashing peace signs to everyone who passed. When cars broke down, and many did, small throngs of people gathered to diagnose and fix the problem, or to generously—and quickly—push them out of the way. Steam billowing thickly from blasted radiators reminded me of an Iron Butterfly concert, and when the dust, smoke (from thousands of lit joints and incense), exhaust fumes, and whiffs of patchouli oil suffused the night air, it made the whole thing seem like some magical journey.

When we finally reached the epicenter of Woodstock, we could hear Richie Havens singing Freedom, emitting his signature sound—singing without dentures. As we meandered through the crowd, kids in psychedelic dance floated around the stage waving bundles of peacock plumes, clearly making no effort to sell them for the capitalist pigs who had supplied them for that purpose. Hari Krishna troupes or brigades, who typically stood out at gatherings of this kind, hovered in groups, jingling their tambourines, chanting their reverential Maha mantra.

By this time, I was both mesmerized and horrified. Where would we go once we passed the stage? What would we drink? (Reference Number 9 on my knowledge of the world list.) Oddly enough, I didn't question where we would find food, even though by now the steaks were floating in melted ice. What bothered me were the sleeping arrangements, and the huge, deafening crowd. What if I got trampled in a rush towards the stage? Where would I shower?

Looking back, of course I realize that I had morphed into a neurotic child of God, which I didn't envision myself as at the time. My freakout amounted to eighteen-year-old paranoia, pure and simple. Nevertheless, the spiral had gained its own momentum, and I begged "my boyfriend" to take me home. For the life of me, I can't remember what I said, or what he said in effort to calm me down and reason with me. I suspect we soon reached the point where I cried, because that usually worked.

So, not long after we arrived after a long and arduous journey, we turned around and left Woodstock, drove twenty miles south, and checked into a motel. I also don't remember much about that, but since it was 1969, I probably slept with him (because Number 7 on the list lessened my fear of Number 6 on the list). The next morning, we pointed the MG in the direction of New York City, and soon spent the rest of that Sunday walking around the eerily quiet Village, telling everyone who would listen that we were at Woodstock. Posters highlighting the many bands that would play (were playing) at the Woodstock festival were plastered on telephone poles and walls, so there was a hint of regret along with the empty boasting.

In truth, I wonder to this day, forty years later, what would have happened had I toughed it out just a bit longer. What's more, I obsess constantly over the fact that the guy I was dating, i.e., "the boyfriend," must tell this story over and over again, calling me "the bitch that made him leave Woodstock."

Michele Hax is a member of the faculty of the Community College of Baltimore County, where she teaches Sociology 101, Racial and Cultural Minorities, Women's Studies, and Women's Self Defense/Violence Against Women. She is a LCSW-C (licensed certified social worker—clinical), who also has a black belt. She considers herself proud to have begun her career in neurosis at Woodstock.

The Search

By Philip Pisani

I scanned the sea of colors, hoping to discover her long, curly, flaming red hair. The hot sun blurred my eyes and the sweet pungent smell of smoke from the clouds of pot stung my nostrils, so I turned away. I thought maybe it was a mistake trekking the six miles from where we parked the car. I turned and looked down at the thousands of people dressed in reds, blues and whites interspersed with mixed flesh tones washed with rain and sun. The hillside looked more like a bowl of Trix than a music festival. Not that I had never been to one.

I tried to hear music, but it was off in the distance, and by the time the notes reached Tom and me, they had collided with back feed from the huge amplifiers and the din of thousands of voices. The whole place was a mess. I expected something different. My excitement in hoping to find her and yet my fear of what I'd find tore through me on my journey to the mount. She was a free woman, the first I knew to go braless. And sex came easy, and it was wild. But now I was afraid of what I would see if I found her. I felt vacant, lost in the thousands of people milling around or bouncing in a form of dance. I stepped into the mass of people sprawled on the mud and grass wandered around as Tom looked on, apparently not wanting to follow.

I picked my way around a guy and a girl both bare from the waist up coupled together in either sleep or unconsciousness. It was hard to tell. I had to watch my footing in some places because of the mud—some of it dried and some still slick with moisture from the rain, spilled water and remaining dew. I stopped and looked around again hoping to spot her and at the same time hoping not to find her if there was a chance of seeing her in some wild state of undress or drug- induced euphoria like many of the people that surrounded me. I found nothing but more of the same.

I walked back to Tom while casting glances around chancing to find Linda. I thought I heard Santana's Soul Sacrifice but was unsure. Santana was one of the few bands I liked, along with Janis Joplin and Jimi Hendrix. I wasn't a music lover. I was a reader. When I got to Tom,

I popped a thin cigar in my mouth and lit it. I wanted the Che look after seeing the movie and reading about him. I wondered if anyone there knew of Che.

"You find her?" Tom asked.

"Nah."

"I can't hear the music," Tom said.

"I know. Plus it's a mess. Whattaya wanna do?"

Tom looked around and shrugged. A longhaired man with a blue and white headband walked past trying to sell us a bag of ice for $1 then defended the price to someone who called him a profiteer.

"Let's walk this way," Tom pointed to section of Hurd Road sloping downward and forming the perimeter of the concert field's west side. People jammed the road going both up and down. Some wobbled as they walked while others wore smiles and swayed in the motion of their movement.

"It's an event," I said walking alongside Tom, my eyes still peeled for red hair. "This is the second place in a few weeks where it's crazy with people."

"Yeah, that's right. You went to the Apollo launch."

"Yeah." I thought back to the rocket pounding into the blue Florida sky and contemplated both events. Man on the moon and man in concert, and all this during a war. I thought of my friend Joe over in Vietnam. "It's all fuckin' crazy," I said to no one as I looked at a guy in a black top hat sitting on the hood of hearse painted every color of the rainbow. The man sat motionless, his eyes glazed. I took a sip of Black Velvet from the flask, then handed it to Tom. "Looks like everyone's stoned or trippin'. And that hearse guy looks dead." Tom also took a shot of the whiskey and handed the flask back. "I don't feel a part of it. I mean the drugs and this sharing. I never tried drugs. I don't see much sharing. And this peace thing. Love and peace. Shit. The country needs a jolt. Not this. We need a Che."

Tom changed the subject. "I heard someone say Canned Heat's next."

"I think we should go back. Go back to the cottage. There are plenty of girls there. I'd rather stay there, maybe get laid."

"Looks like you can get laid here pretty easy," Tom said.

I thought of Linda. "Yeah, but let's go anyway." I was afraid that was what I'd find, Linda with another guy and nude or something like that.

We headed up Hurd Road in the direction of Route 97 to Tom's car, five miles away. We passed more of the same. People warned others coming towards them to turn back, that it wasn't worth it. I walked on in silence thinking about Che.

Phil Pisani's work appeared in The Long Trip Home, Small Spiral Notebook, Ragazine, and other e-zines. He is co-author of the book From Heroin to Heresy: The Making of an American Social Hero. He continues to write novels, short stories, and screenplays.

Susan Reynolds

To be French and Born Again in America
By Francis Dumaurier

August 10, 1969. I'm flying from Paris to JFK with my friend Loïc. We're excited about discovering the land of rock n' roll. It's our first trip to the States and we're the first of our group of friends to cross the Atlantic. We land to refuel in Canada and, as we wait, a young guy asks us if we're going to Woodstock. This event is news to us, but we're instantly interested—after all, we've just seen Monterey Pop and Easy Rider in Parisian theaters to prepare for our great American adventure.

Mark comes to pick us up at JFK to drive us to his cousin David's house, where we can stay until we take a bus to San Francisco. We met Mark and David when they visited Europe during the summer of 1967 and stayed in touch by mail.

Honky Tonk Women is the first song we hear on the radio on our way to Manhattan, where we walk to Central Park and, unbelievable but true, Jefferson Airplane is giving a free concert on the grass. The buzz is: next weekend - Woodstock. David offers to arrange for tickets and carpooling through a local FM radio station, if we're interested. Interested??? Like we have better things to do???

Back at David's house we listen to The Band's Big Pink and The Beach Boys' 20/20; later, we visit his friends to hear The Who's Tommy in its entirety.

We have tickets for Saturday and Sunday. We meet our hosts on Friday night and six of us cram in a white Mustang convertible. We sit like sardines, and we don't mind the drizzle as we ride on the New York State Thruway until we get stuck in traffic . . . literally . . . in the middle of the Thruway. So, Loïc, David, and I thank our gracious hosts and start walking through the fields toward a country road where traffic is slow but moving. We find a ride, sit in the car, and the rain starts pouring.

As we move like snails, we hear on the car radio that, because of the weather, the concert is canceled and the governor has officially declared the place a disaster area, asking one and all to return to where they came from. We look at each other and ponder what to do. I tell Loïc that, since

40

I'm so close to the place, I have to see the stage even if the concert is canceled and the place closed.

Loïc decides to come with me on the long walk to Max Yasgur's farm. Luckily, the rain has stopped, and the sun is peeking through. Along the way, people are amazingly friendly, giving us biscuits and water.

We finally enter the arena. What an amazing site. On my first day in America, I get to see Jefferson Airplane in the park. Now, on my first weekend ever in America, I join a sea of kindred spirits on another planet. I know right away that I'm where I belong.

My favorite moments: Mountain's thunderous aural attack, Canned Heat's Boogie at night while small fires are burning on the hills, waking up to the unmistakable voice of Janis Joplin, falling asleep after The Who's complete performance of Tommy, awakening to the call of Grace Slick at the crack of dawn, Alvin Lee's false start and fiery version of Going Home, Carlos Santana's hot dance beat, CSN&Y's melodic but humble beginnings, John Sebastian's dreamy touch, Joe Cocker belting it out as the storm gathers strength, waking up to The Paul Butterfield Blues band's unscheduled performance, standing in disbelief in a field of wet muddy garbage as Jimi Hendrix plays a very long set to a much smaller crowd while a girl keeps screaming "Voodoo Chile, I want Voodoo Chile" until he finally obliges . . .

The time has come to leave the site, and a state trooper asks us if we need a ride. He stops a car and asks the driver to drop us at the Monticello bus depot. In Manhattan, we take the C train to David's Upper West Side apartment. People on the subway are reading daily papers with headlines like "3 Days of Drugs, Sex, and Rock n' Roll." We stand beaming, a little frazzled, covered with mud. People are watching us as if we are zombies.

In December, four months after Woodstock, I go to the Altamont speedway to see The Rolling Stones' free concert, which is already called "Woodstock West." It's a disaster, but I am happy to have come and witnessed in person how Woodstock came and went, and why it can never be duplicated.

When the artificial re-creation of Woodstock is planned in 1994, I contact all the media of New York City to speak against this fallacy.

Nobody returns my calls, the event is a dud, and I hope it never happens again.

I passed a masters degree in American studies at the University of Paris in 1971 and eventually became a proud American citizen twenty-five years ago. Woodstock is where my current life started and the original program of the event is framed, along with my very own concert and muddy emergency food tickets, on the wall facing me.

There were no drugs and sex for me, but there was plenty of rock 'n roll. The most important is that I was there and that I remember everything— a heck of a field trip!

Francis Dumaurier is an actor who works in the French and English languages. He is a member of SAG, AFTRA, and AEA and has lived in New York City since 1977. More information is available on his website at www.francisdumaurier.com.

How I Spent My Summer Vacation

By Louis S. Denaro

I was traveling with my parents and younger siblings to a resort near Swan Lake on August 15, 1969, when we got tied up in the bizarre traffic jam on Route 17B leading into Bethel. Assorted transistor radios provided the soundtrack as a sea of headlights captured rain-soaked hippies, in various stages of dress, romping through the traffic or throwing rolls of toilet paper through the air or sitting on the backs of vehicles with their little pipes blowing bubbles and/or other things. One merry band pushed a love bus up a slope alongside the road until gravity pulled it down towards traffic, repeating this process over and over again. Things got really intense when our sorry little 1963 Plymouth sedan broke down in the middle of the road, and my very visibly upset father had to abandon us and wait in an extremely long line at a pay phone to get help.

In his absence, an ambulance crept up behind us. Imagine the trauma we wide-eyed children in the back seat experienced when a hippie girl challenged my mother:

Hysterical waif-like Hippie Girl, with hair down to her bottom, yells, "Lady, you have to move this car!" forces her way in, grabs the keys, turns the ignition, and nothing happens.

Petrified Fascist-Italy born/bred Long Island hausfrau, with modified-beehive, shrieks (with Italian accent), "my husband no here, my husband no here," repeatedly hits intrusive girl over the head with her umbrella.[END EXT]

Salvation ultimately appeared when the girl's boyfriend dragged her away, and he and his friends tried to push our car off the road. The ambulance finally snaked around us, and Pop returned just as a nurse pulled up to give us the jump that got our car running again. When the radio reported someone had been run over and was being taken to the hospital in critical condition, we surmised a bubble-blowing hippie fell off the back of a car.

Pop's relief at finding someone in authority turned to outrage when the very same cop directing traffic at the cloverleaf near Monticello Raceway told us we couldn't use 17B and turned us completely around, which meant spending more hours heading in the wrong direction. But Pop's screams didn't begin to compare with the performance my mother delivered when we arrived at our destination seven hours late, and the unsympathetic owner informed her that he gave our rooms away—to the state cops. Not exactly the ideal beginning to a relaxing family weekend getaway.

When they discovered that our resort was only several miles from the actual concert site, the grown-ups quickly adopted a siege mentality. The paranoia started when it became obvious that our hosts were running low on food. The refugee-like atmosphere wasn't helped by the sight of empty shelves in Monticello stores; except for a toy machine gun that my dad purchased so that I could project imaginary fire through our car windows at the rows of hippies on each side of the road while he gave them dirty looks from behind the wheel.

In contrast, I had it made. Where else could I choose between spending an hour watching "Dark Shadows" or riding on a state trooper's motorcycle? And how awesome was it to spend nights checking out the sounds echoing through the Mongaup Valley while the rotating Sullivan County Airport beacon served as my own private light show? Or hearing the jukebox endlessly repeat "Sweet Caroline" while sipping my Seven-Up straight from the bottle and alternately watching the adults fight and the hippies hike up the street to come in and use the phone or the bathroom or get something to eat or whatever. It was wonderful.

On the way home from Swan Lake, both sides of the road were lined with rows of hippies and their signs, and my dad actually slowed the car down, lowered the window, put his left arm out the window, and made a certain gesture. Mom tried to convince him to rein it in, but Dad resisted. I did my part—mowing down hippies with my toy machine gun.

In hindsight, my mother may have been the one most affected by our Woodstock experience. Personally witnessing a happening where so many people could freely express themselves, particularly in stark contrast to her wartime upbringing in a regime that instilled fear and suppressed personal freedom, apparently raised her consciousness. Our Hallmark moment came a year later when she and I spied a Woodstock movie poster and cracked up laughing without a single word passing between us. Within a year, she got U.S. citizenship and a driver's license, but she was on her way to real independence when she proclaimed that hippies were cool and partnered with a neighbor to open a boutique that sold love beads and mood rings and consequently incorporated these items into her daily wardrobe. Her newly acquired life balance and idealism affected most of us—with the exception of my father, who still seems to be taking his time managing these social transitions.

On August 15, 2008, Pop and I happened to be driving upstate on Route 17B for the first time since 1969, and when I started reminiscing, we soon realized that the festival had begun thirty-nine years ago on that very day. So, of course I wanted to pull off onto 17B to retrace our circuitous route in its entirety. When Pop realized I was serious about this, a look of terror flashed over his face. He looked like he might have a seizure. "Louie, I don't know what you were thinking back then, but I'm not going back there. This place brings back baaaaddd memories," he said. The edginess and paranoia were as real on that day as they were in 1969, because where my pop's concerned, it will always be August 15, 1969, in that neck of the woods . . . now wouldn't that be a dream come true.

Louis Salvatore Denaro believes his Woodstock experience may have helped drive his decision to mike up his French horn and play it in rock bands over the past twenty years. His initials are not a put-on, affectation or legacy of his sixties experience; rather they come from the Sicilian tradition of being named after both grandfathers, which in his case worked out as LSD. This is his first attempt at writing a submission intended for publication.

Grooving on the Weekends

By Rozanne Reynolds

Ascribed as a teenager to care for an older sister slowly dying of cancer, I coped by fantasizing about freedom. I dreamt of traveling the world, and I might have gone that route, had I not heeded my mother's advice to attend secretarial school, so I "would always have something to fall back on." Even in those liberating days, schools and parents primarily groomed girls to become housewives, teachers, librarians, nurses, or secretaries. After a boring freshman year, I bolted, moved back home—and felt trapped all over again.

I then opted for airline school, dreaming of quite literally taking flight. Alas, my sense of loyalty led me to decline offers when my best friend couldn't land a job at the same airline. Instead, we both took jobs at Hertz-Rent-a-Car in New York City, where I became, of course, a secretary.

Monday through Friday, I conformed, wearing makeup, dresses, nylons, and heels. On weekends, I dressed like the hippie I longed to be, replete with really low-cut, extreme bellbottoms—frayed at the hem—long "love" beads, beaded headbands, and funky sandals. I would hop on the subway to Manhattan to attend peace rallies in Central Park, or out to Rockaway Beach to hang with real hippies.

As the Vietnam War escalated, rallies drew larger and larger crowds, and I loved grooving to music, shouting slogans, and carrying placards urging everyone to "make love not war." Since my older brother had gone to Vietnam and came home a different person—newly and deeply introspective, withdrawn, and increasingly morose—I didn't want my younger brother, Roy, to go to Vietnam too. I didn't want any more American boys to die for a war that made no sense.

My sister Susan came to New York for the summer, and when we saw ads for the Woodstock Music & Art Fair, we talked Roy into hitching up from Pennsylvania to join us. But we had one problem: None of us had a car and we were all too young to rent a car. Luckily, I had begun dating Tom, a Vietnam vet, who was old enough to rent a car.

Unfortunately, Tom had a litany of concerns: "It will be insanely crowded (we had no idea), it's supposed to rain (we had no idea), there won't be any place to sit (ditto) . . . " When I told Tom we'd hitchhike to Woodstock, he agreed to take us, but issued orders: "We can't possibly leave until after work Friday night, and we have to come back Sunday so we all can get to work on time Monday." Susan, Roy, and I wanted to go so badly, we agreed.

Friday night we headed north toward Woodstock, with no real idea of what we would encounter, but who cared? Peace and love vibes coursed through my body like a drumbeat. The closer we got the more my heart raced. For three days, I could be with people who cared more about their beliefs than how they looked; people who embraced freedom; people who were non-judgmental; people who loved music—my people.

Miles before the exit, abandoned cars lined the Thruway. A policeman waved us over, told us the road was closed, and urged us to go home. I turned to Tom, and pleaded, "Let's not give up, please. We can walk from here. Or, can't we find another way in?" Susan and Roy also pleaded, until Tom finally acquiesced. It was already raining so we slept in the car, and the next morning doubled back to a small town where a storeowner told us another way in.

Somehow we split up, and Tom and I worked our way down until we were in front of the stage. (We're visible on the album cover). Once settled on our patch of mud, I breathed deeply and allowed the music and the ambiance to wash over me—drifting blissfully into my own little world, surrounded by young people yearning for peace and love and nothing (that day) more than fantastic music and a chance to let our hair down. Since I had a lighter, people began coming to me to light their joints, offering joints and/or drags in return.

I turned around often to gaze at the crowd and found it awe-inspiring that such a massive group of people could get along in those conditions—hot sun, rain, hot sun, thundershowers, mud, little to no food or water, few and smelly portable-potties. A few times, when the crowd roared, like when Country Joe MacDonald sang his rousing anti-war song, a shiver ran through me, a shiver of recognition that my generation was passionately against war and death and destruction and racism and forcing ourselves to be like everyone else. And that it was an occasion to celebrate, because we were something to behold.

47

As night encroached, I begged Tom to hold out long enough to see The Who, scheduled to perform at midnight. Tom held out until 4:30 A.M., but then insisted we go back to the car so he could sleep. Susan and Roy were there when we arrived, and although everyone else somehow managed to sleep, my brain was spinning, my heart racing. I couldn't help thinking: My world, my people lay just over the hill.

Unfortunately, when we awoke the next morning, it was raining again, and Tom insisted that we leave to "beat the traffic." Who cared about traffic? I felt devastated. Tom was the only one who wanted to leave, and he was driving. And so we left Woodstock, one of the best times of my life.

I went back to Queens, back to my secretarial job, and back to Central Park on the weekends. I married Tom, moved to Long Island, had two (adorable) children, and spent fifteen years teaching Montessori school, before becoming a legal secretary, and eventually a paralegal . . . and sometimes I wonder if it was what I would have chosen, if I hadn't felt compelled to please my mother, my friend, or Tom, more than myself.

If Susan, Roy, and I had hitched to Woodstock, we would have gone Thursday and stayed through to the end. I would have swam naked in the pond and been hungry often, and totally exhausted. Perhaps I would have finally unleashed the hippie I longed to become . . . and who knows what would have happened next?

Rozanne Reynolds was a suburban earth mother in the 70s and later a single mother who focused most of her energy on raising her beloved Michele and Christopher. Nearing retirement, she is cutting back on her paralegal hours and spending a lot more time seeking a new life, a new form of expression, something closer, perhaps, to what the hippie girl inside her would like to do. She lives in North Carolina, and has adopted and nurtured multiple abused dogs as pets, including Skip, Princess, Obie, and Zena, who is deaf. This is her first published story.

By the Time They Got to Woodstock,

I was Already There

By Jeff Blumenfeld

Max Yasgur was a customer of my father's clothing store in Monticello, just ten miles from the site of the Woodstock Music and Art Fair. Two years after the festival, when I was a student reporter for the Syracuse New Times, an alternative weekly newspaper at Syracuse University, I prevailed upon Yasgur, my fellow Monticello High School graduate (albeit thirty-one years apart), to tell me how the festival came about despite fierce local opposition.

Yasgur remembered how some Sullivan County elders were outraged at his agreement to rent land to Woodstock entrepreneurs Michael Lang and John Roberts.

"Don't buy Yasgur's milk. He loves hippies," read two signs bordering his property before the festival. Several customers switched milk companies and he was threatened personally.

At one of the last town board meetings held before the event, Yasgur defended his plan to county and state safety officials.

Yasgur asked each official if there were any stipulations within their departments that hadn't been met to accommodate the expected 40,000 people per day. When no reservations were raised, he addressed the entire meeting: "So the only objection to having a festival here is to keep longhairs out of town?"

A murmur of dissent swept through the heavily conservative Republican crowd, and Yasgur bellowed: "Well, you can all go pound salt up your ass, because come August 15 we're going to have a festival!" He stormed out of the room and the rest became rock history.

It was the defining moment of my generation. Four hundred thousand-plus baby boomers were making a pilgrimage to Yasgur's farm. It seemed as if the world was coming to my back yard. This was the biggest thing to happen to the county, well, ever. Certainly bigger than Frank Sinatra, Milton Berle and Don Rickles playing the now closed Concord and Grossinger's hotels.

Three days of peace and music with some of the greatest bands of all time. People my age were having sex with strangers, I was sure of it. And what did I do? I left after two hours.

"Too crowded," I told my mother later that Friday night.

I was hot, thirsty, and within minutes became separated from my friends. By the time I decided that I was out of there, I managed to find Freddie Rausch's mother, the neighbor who had kindly dropped me off and had plenty of room in her car to take me back to Monticello.

But the story doesn't end there for my sorry self, who still regrets, now almost forty years later, that he heard not a note of music, smelled not a whiff of grass, didn't even see a naked woman.

I was one of those small town kids who used to hang out at the local firehouse on weekends. I worked on an ambulance and was a ham operator. Others my age, I was sure, were surfing off Malibu, meeting tall and tan girls in Ipanema, or salsa dancing in Miami discos. Me? I was "talking" in dots and dashes to other nerds somewhere out in the ether.

Just back from the festival site that first evening, I dropped by one of my teenage haunts—the Civil Defense headquarters in the county courthouse where, as a volunteer, I was allowed to talk to truckers, delivery people, and assorted oddballs who had CB base stations in their homes.

I logged on and was swamped with requests from mobile CB operators in the vicinity of the Bethel festival site. I was dispatching emergency calls for water and drugs, relaying messages from authorities, and calling nervous parents by telephone to tell them their kids were fine, if not a bit freaked out by the crowds. In fact, I was one of the few links between the Yasgur farm site and town. The phones were overloaded, and emergency services were taxed to the breaking point.

At precisely 5 P.M. the Civil Defense secretary said, "I'm leaving." I pleaded with her to stay but instead, she said that there was no need to stay because, "They're hippies. They don't need any water." She was half-joking, of course, but left anyway.

I continued to work the radio well into that Friday night, eventually developing a strain in my thumb from holding down the "talk" button. I returned the next day until I could stand it no longer and by that Saturday afternoon handed off my post to another volunteer.

The local newspaper was beside itself, as you can imagine, that this hippie tsunami had rolled through the county, clogged roads, crammed festival medical tents with drug overdoses, and Civil Defense decided to "go home," leaving the office in the hands of a seventeen-year-old radio operator.

Yasgur recalled that in the years that followed the festival, it was hard to keep a sign in front of his dairy farm because anything with his name on it became a collector's item. He became almost a patron saint, and was called the "Father of the Woodstock Nation." He turned down an appearance on To Tell the Truth, but agreed to an interview on The Merv Griffin Show, "just to see what it would be like." For that Syracuse newspaper story, the strong-willed Yasgur told me that he could have become a rich man in those post-Woodstock days. Hip entrepreneurs often approached him with one scheme or another: Yasgur-for-President t-shirts, the national roll-out of his milk, offering empty milk cartons with his name on it, and selling Yasgur posters. "I'll be god-damned if I'll capitalize on what was an accident," the strong-willed farmer said.

A community that once even fought a historical state marker on the site has rethought its Woodstock legacy. High unemployment, the shuttering of once world famous resort hotels and the lack of state approval for Vegas-style casino gambling to help bail out the economy has made the $100 million Bethel Woods Center for the Arts, an outdoor performing arts center and museum that opened in 2008, an economic lifesaver for an otherwise depressed region.

Max Yasgur died of a heart ailment on Feb. 8, 1973, at the age of fifty-three. "Woodstock was no achievement for Max," his wife said. "The festival was just an extraordinary event that widened his experience in life because of his contact with these people."

Jeff Blumenfeld runs a public relations agency in Darien, Conn., www.blumenfeldpr.com. His Max Yasgur newspaper article can be seen at www.yasgurroad.com/landsale.html. And despite his best efforts, Jeff's friends still ask him how he liked Woodstock.

The Wheels on the Bus

By Sandra Johnson

My friend likes to tell me that life is a series of intersecting circles akin to one repeating cosmic Venn diagram. For me, that elliptical center where all experiences intersect has always been music. You see, my Dad was a musician in the 1940s and although the only remnant of that period in my life is a faded black and white playbill and the memory of a worn violin on a piano top, music has always been my lifeblood.

So, when an opportunity was announced for three tickets to a nearby "folk festival" in the Catskills, my two friends and I were hooked. We were three university students cemented somewhere between "sophomore slump" and declaring our majors in selfless employment in order to save the planet. It was August 1969, and we were suffering immeasurable boredom working on an assembly line at Eastman Kodak in Rochester, New York.

With little concern for life, limb, or paycheck, we headed to the mountains for the opening of the Woodstock Music & Art Fair. It was dark when we arrived at Yasgur's farm, so we unpacked sleeping bags and claimed a spot overlooking the stage. My first and clearest memory is waking up next to thousands of strangers. The reunion of strangers began, and we all shared whatever we could find: bits of food, cigarettes, money, and directions. With recognizing smiles and congratulatory hugs, we scanned the meadow and began what was later chronicled as "breakfast in bed for 400,000."

The first order of business was to locate my boyfriend. We were scheduled to meet Friday at the Aquarian parking lot. After visiting the first, then the second, I realized with a heavy heart that each lot bore the Aquarian title. Miraculously, while wandering from lot to lot, I heard my name called. He said he recognized me from the back, which, forty years later, is a detail worth noting.

The mere presence of the emerging population leveled the gates and the need for tickets moot. We happily found a spot for our blanket and began the adventure of a lifetime. We suddenly knew that this was not just a historic musical event; this was a social cataclysm, a lawless, drug-assisted, rebellious human soup. From coeds to drug pushers, the young and old, unborn and reborn, having no common goal or politic, we formed a city, shared our space, danced to our own choreography and instantly became headline news. Amid the aromas of bonfires and contact highs, clothed and unclothed, we suddenly became a family of music worshipers.

But then, the mercury rose, the beat intensified, rain fell and civility turned to excitement, excitement to lack of convention, playfulness to hedonism. This was no place for the daughter of a violinist. And so, with soggy resolve, mud-caked shoes and fond V-shaped farewells, my boyfriend and I began the long trek away from this reservation called Woodstock Nation. Lining our pathway were miles of incoming vehicles, curious bystanders, enterprising children selling water, bananas, and lemonade, tired and hungry rock refugees inhabiting open-doored motel rooms and abandoned cars. At our lowest, hungriest and dirtiest moment, a group called to us from a motel swimming pool and invited us for pizza and a shower. The common denominator among us was the event. If you had been, admission was free.

We headed to the Nevele Hotel in Ellenville. My boyfriend's family was spending a relaxing weekend in the Catskills and with "you must be kidding" written on their faces, they invited us to their room for food, a shower, and of course, the use of a phone. It was time to call my dad and chat musician to musician.

I would now try to explain that things were changing, that music had taken on a more serious tone. Something really important was brewing. I would try to tell him that living peacefully alongside nearly a half-million people had changed my parochial thinking. Perhaps it's what happens to people who survive an accidental brush with greatness. For me, it took my ordinary life and lifted it to higher ground, to a mental landscape where music again carried the message of social change. I truly believed that we would overcome. I agreed with words like, "War, what is it good for?" The music made me braver, more willing to step outside the norm.

The inclusive spirit of Woodstock supported my fledgling resolve to move outside my comfort zone. I married that Jewish boy from Long Island and some years later lived in a converted school bus. We started a free school in Cleveland and lived communally for a year. We applied to the Peace Corps and drove cross-country in a rusty VW Beetle. We had a son and named him for an Old Testament hero from Jericho. I embraced my adopted Jewishness and learned the Sabbath prayers. I believed that life can be reinvented at any time. I still do. You are the composer and conductor and thus decide what key of life to live. I choose major over minor whenever I can.

And now I am fifty-eight and my heart still beats faster to Dylan's earliest poetry, to Richie Havens's idea of a great Mandela. I still sing and the circles may swing wide to Beethoven and Brahms, but at the center of my Venn history, there is all music that soothes and elevates. The wheels on the bus began with words of peace, but gave way to freedom buses in Mississippi and the seeds of integration. And for me, through every open window along the American road, I hear a song.

Sandra Johnson is a retired teacher of thirty-four years. She began her career running a free school in Cleveland, Ohio, then taught special education in Wilton, Ridgefield and Washington, Connecticut. She continues to sing with the Connecticut Master Chorale and enjoys sharing her life experiences with six grandchildren. She does not play violin but her dad has long forgiven her for her musical roots firmly embedded in folk music and sixties rock.

Peace and Music in Wartime

By Bob Brown

I grew up in a working class neighborhood, in the mainly blue-collar city of Hamilton, Ontario, an hour from the border. I was the youngest of four in a Catholic home, and thus the recipient of strong moral guidance. Far from being a hippie, I developed a disdain for the drug culture—sports and music became my drugs of choice. My first live musical experience occurred in a church auditorium, listening to a band fronted by David Clayton-Thomas, later of Blood, Sweat, & Tears fame. I was hooked.

In August of '69 I had just turned nineteen after completing my first year college, and was working in a funeral home for the summer. Short hair required. My friends and I had missed the Atlantic City festival, so when we saw an ad for a "White Lake Music Festival" and saw that Sly & the Family Stone and The Who would be there, we jumped on board.

Our journey to this cultural milestone did not go as planned, much like the festival itself. In retrospect it included a wonderful sequence of haphazard events. First, after arguing with my boss, I quit. We left early Friday, filled with anticipation. On the approach to the Lewiston Bridge, we picked up a hitchhiker. Turns out he had already been turned away once, which led to guilt by association from a customs agent, who sneered, "You freaks going to the freak festival," and then turned us away. No worries, off to the Rainbow Bridge.

En route, however, we got rear ended, but soldiered on. At the Rainbow Bridge, a customs agent said, "Open the trunk." But the accident had inflicted too much damage. Borrowing some tools from fellow travelers, we removed the back seat, and two hours later, the agent finally sent us on our way. God bless America.

Arrival in the dark of night was surreal. Parking miles from the site, we wandered through a dark mist toward the stage, so dark we almost walked into people, some clothed, some naked, many wet, stoned, and tired. Then sounds and spotlights in the distance, and in a few more minutes we were there. I could hear Melanie singing, but had to follow the spotlights down to the stage to find her. Next, Arlo Guthrie talked about seeing "a lot of freaks" in the audience, and Joan Baez spoke of her activist husband's incarceration. The anti-war emotions were palpable.

Throughout the weekend, the peace message rang loud and clear. As an outsider, I hadn't appreciated the American counterculture's anger toward an unwanted war, their fear of being called to duty, or facing the prospect of a loved one being involuntarily shipped to a foreign land, never to return. Forty years later, as the parent of a nineteen-year-old son and a countryman mourning the loss of soldiers in Afghanistan, I now understand their activism and their burning desire for peace and love to annihilate war.

Forty years later, images remain embedded forever in my psyche: Bob "The Bear" of Canned Heat holding a microphone in one hand, lifting a cameraman with his other arm; Mountain's larger than life Leslie West playing a guitar that looked child-size next to his body; Santana's Soul Sacrifice enveloping the countryside; waking up in the middle of the night and, quite by chance, catching a classic performance by Sly & the Family Stone . . . and sheets of rain showering down.

As the sun fell on Sunday, we returned to our battered vehicle, where a turn of the key launched another adventure—it wouldn't start. Figuring no one would pick up four guys, I split from my friends, and headed to a fountain to clean up. A hulking NBC cameraman was shooting images for the rest of the world to see. Ignoring him, and then leaving most of my belongings behind, I headed home.

Luckily, I scored rides from Yasgur's farm to Liberty to Rochester, and then after catching a bus to Buffalo, scored another ride across the Peace Bridge, and finally, and most memorably, a ride from Fort Erie in a carnival truck. I had to ride those last sixty miles with my right arm out the window clutching a door that wouldn't lock, and one eye on the gas cap that kept falling off. Entering downtown Hamilton Monday morning, I arrived in a vehicle more beaten up than the one left behind.

Walking the last mile home I felt strangely rejuvenated, a new person, a citizen of the world. I had come from a place where status and material things meant nothing, and hatred and violence didn't exist. I couldn't wait to get home to tell everyone about my odyssey.

That evening I watched the Buffalo NBC station. As coverage turned to what the world would come to know as Woodstock, there I was at the fountain, many miles away, washing away the muddy remnants of three glorious days that will never happen again.

Bob Brown is a marketing specialist with a large international plastics company, living in Burlington, Ontario. He dedicates his story to his father Victor, a part-time freelance writer to whom he is forever grateful for letting him go to Woodstock, and to his son Michael who probably thinks his dad didn't leave Woodstock completely behind him.

I had to Go

By John Northlake

As soon as I saw that brochure at a little bookstore in St. Louis, I knew right away: I had to go to this mega-concert in upstate New York. I had to go. I knew my parents wouldn't mind because they had no idea of the magnitude or the significance of this event. Neither did I. That summer in 1969, while I was busy trimming grass around tombstones in historic Bellefontaine Cemetery, the underground rock music scene was reaching its peak.

The fact that our generation owned the music was very important, to say the least. My parents had their old favorites, like wartime tunes and hymns, but that reflected a nostalgic past that was totally meaningless to me. Our music was an essential part of our lives. It defined us as a movement, a unique culture that was for us and no one else. It was like a secret language, unbeknownst to the elders.

My love of music began with classical music. After seeing the Disney movie, I insisted my parents buy me the "Fantasia" LP with glossy versions of Igor Stravinsky's Rite of Spring and Bach's dramatic Toccata and Fugue in D Minor. That record had such an impact on me that at age twelve, I decided that music was the most important thing in my life.

In high school, after hearing the Kingston Trio singing songs that told stories, and Peter, Paul and Mary singing protest songs by Bob Dylan, folk music became our thing. After trying to learn folk from a book of Joan Baez songs, I had to accept the fact that I was not going to be the next Pete Seeger. But it was the message in the songs that transcended the singers and had a profound impact on what was to come.

When rock and folk joined forces, things really changed. When I heard the Byrds' version of Turn, Turn, Turn, I knew right away that was the real thing. Now there was a reason to listen to the radio. Now the commerciality of rock and roll was at least partially transformed into music with a purpose. Dylan broke the rules of folk music and conveniently became the subject of my high school poetry presentation, complete with music. The flow of new groups came quickly. By the time

I started college in 1967, my record collection included the Doors, Jethro Tull, Buffalo Springfield, Jefferson Airplane, Hendrix, and the Dead. All underground rockers at the time.

My experience at Yasgur's farm was exciting and miserable at the same time. Completely unprepared, my friend Pete Faur and I walked off the bus, saw that the fence was down, put our tickets back in our pockets and hunkered down at the back of the most massive crowd I had ever seen. Later that evening I stood up and looked back. We were now in the middle of a crowded mass of humanity that was truly unbelievable. No one complained about the rain, the heat, the rain, the lack of food, the mud, the rain. In spite of the unpleasant conditions, we were all a bunch of happy clams having the greatest time of our lives, drugs or no drugs, food or no food. At one point Pete volunteered to go look for food. Two hours later, he returned with only two cold hot dogs. Friendly people around us passed joints and bottles of wine. Sleeping was nearly impossible, but I do remember snoozing some before dawn. And the rain . . . .

There was no heavy media coverage like there would have been today. This was more of a private event; we were just there for the music and the peace-promoting culture it had spawned. The gathering grew into an event that defined a generation, as they say. Best announcement: "We're now the third largest city in the state of New York, man!" The music that we heard was good, but the event itself overshadowed the performances in my opinion. Best lead-in: "Gimme an F!"

Although Pete and I didn't stay the whole weekend, just the experience of having been at Woodstock was special. I feel historically connected to the other fans, the groups and the locals. Even leaving was an experience. Everyone was willing to help. We hitched a ride on a Good Humor Ice Cream truck, hanging onto the sides. A kind lady let us ride on the top of her station wagon. When we made it back to Manhattan, people came up to us like we were rock stars. I guess there had been some media coverage after all. Topping it off was finding a room at the rather sleazy Woodstock Hotel near Times Square late that night.

If I hadn't dropped in at that little bookstore, I probably would have missed the festival and regretted it. Luckily, I didn't miss it, and it's become one of my life's major milestones. Even though it's now widespread and often over-commercialized, I still consider pop music to be important and vital as an art, much more than just an ear-plugged soundtrack to our busy lives.

John Northlake graduated from the University of Missouri-Columbia with a degree in photojournalism and has worked in photography, advertising, and printing. He now resides in Orlando, Florida, and has three children with his wife, Julie. A longtime audiophile, John still strives to own the most musical two-channel audio system within monetary limits.

Bob Dylan: AWOL or MIA?

By Geraldine Goldberg

"Bob Dylan, Bobby Dylan, come out, come out wherever you are." Long before the Woodstock festival, my friends and I had driven to Dylan's hometown, where we joyfully sang that taunt over and over until a shopkeeper in the tiny town of Woodstock politely asked us to quit. We were free-spirited, simply pure, and openly naïve teenagers, but by nightfall, Dylan had not shown up, and we left feeling disappointed that we had driven all the way to Dylan's town and not hung out with Dylan.

In 1969 I was twenty-one years old. Richard Nixon had been elected president the previous November, and that horrifying event, along with the escalation of violence in Vietnam, sparked a revolution on college campuses nationwide, including the University of Bridgeport, where I was a student. I was beginning to form ideas about the war and society in general. For me, Richard Nixon personified all that was wrong in the world.

Early that spring I spent time on the campus at Yale, where the politics and the psychedelics were more intense. One evening, during a film festival, I watched the Dylan documentary Don't Look Back and was spellbound. As I exited the theater, I experienced an epiphany, a revelation wherein I witnessed a glimpse into the infinite cosmic scheme of things. I thought the next time I'd see Dylan would be at the Woodstock Festival. Since it was taking place in his back yard, I assumed he'd be there . . . of course he would perform. I bought my ticket.

Six of us decided to go together, too many for one car, so I drove my 1962 black Volkswagen Beetle, and my friend Bev drove her mom's big gray battleship. Three others went with Bev in the ship, and a guy, whose name I don't remember, rode with me in the VW. We left Connecticut in tandem early Thursday morning. A few hours later we came to the crossroads near Bethel, New York, where traffic officers waved my VW ahead. From the rearview mirror I saw the ship had been stopped. We never saw Bev and her shipmates again. At the concert site a day early, we easily found a parking place in a nearby field, and then we headed over to check things out. We were absolutely blown away by the size of the enormous scaffolding, the countless huge black amplifiers, and the massive stage. Groovy roadies and flirtatious groupies were buzzing around everywhere, and the sweet, sweet smell of marijuana permeated the air. The festival had not even begun yet. What a scene!

We slept crammed in the VW that night, and early Friday morning we grabbed our gear and walked right up in front of the stage and remained there for Friday's entire show. We spread our blankets edge to edge with those of other festival attendees. It was one great big party. Everything was perfect: the music, the dancing, the drugs, the hugs, the laughter, the feeling of community, even the eventual rain. What else could we need, except Bob Dylan?

But by Saturday morning, the lack of Dylan, along with too much rain dampened my spirits. After sloshing about in the mud and feeling the effect of too many drugs and too little sleep, I decided to leave. The guy decided to stay, and he and a couple others pushed my VW out of the mud. Since the New York State Thruway was closed, I had to drive to Pennsylvania to reach Interstate 95 for the rest of my trip home to Connecticut.

Back in 1969, I went to Woodstock for the music, and yet now, forty years later, it's strange to admit that the music is not so much what I recall. Maybe that's because Dylan wasn't there. What I do fondly recall is the freewheeling spirit of folks working together for peace through music, as well as the unimaginable camaraderie of thousands of strangers creating a community.

"Where the '60s meet the sea" is the motto of the small coastal community in northern California where I live today. We are activists, entrepreneurs, educators, homesteaders, farmers, intellectuals, craftspeople, and artists, many of us still living the counter-culture lifestyle. Our town is a nuclear-free zone. We've had a Green Party majority on our city council, and we've been a sanctuary for war resisters. We have raised our children to walk gently on Mother Earth.

To this day, I still have not hung out with Dylan. But as a longtime community radio volunteer, I have entertained countless listeners with his music. I always get phone calls at the station when playing a Dylan tune, and then I know he and I have touched a chord in someone's life. I have a young friend, a fellow radio activist, who loves hearing stories about Woodstock. I smile each time he introduces me to one of his contemporaries: "This is Geraldine . . . she was at Woodstock."

Geraldine Goldberg is a community activist, with a passion for gardening. At the age of fifty she received a master's degree with distinction in sociology from Humboldt State University. Her thesis, "I Have Given up My Society World Self: Self and Other in the Julia Butterfly Tapes" remains popular among local environmentalists.

I Still Remember Him

The Story Of Fred Cannock, Retired Senior Investigator BCI – NYSP

By Michele Starkey

As a senior investigator for the New York State Police Bureau of Criminal Investigations, I had seen my fair share of drug-related busts. The 1960s were, after all, fertile ground for just about any illegal drug contraband that you could imagine. Drugs were everywhere, even in rural America.

Yet, even with its ever-growing drug culture, the rural farmland in Sullivan County, New York, did not draw large crowds of people. We rarely ever saw anyone of any notoriety. So, it was quite an undertaking for the small group of New York State Police officers to monitor and control the crowds that swelled to the hundreds of thousands for the gathering in Woodstock in August of 1969.

Our unit was immediately placed on twelve-hour shifts. To discuss our plan of action, some of us decided to stop at the Holiday Inn to have a few cocktails the evening before the concert was scheduled to begin. Just as I was about to swallow my first sip of gin and tonic, a buzz ignited in the room, and we watched an entourage saunter through the door and up to the bar.

Her hair was tousled and teased, a cigarette dangled from her lips and rows of bangle bracelets clanged as she swung a leg up and over the barstool. They were a loud and unruly bunch, and I spotted him then, tall, dark-skinned, clad in leather pants and a leather vest. He stood behind her and leaned in to check out the whiskey on the shelves before pointing to the Jack Daniels bottle. The bartender placed the bottle on the bar, along with a handful of shot glasses. Several of the guys with them were surveying the crowd and deadlocked eyes with us. One of men pointed us out to the tall fellow, who merely smirked and shook his head. There were just four of us, and fourteen of them. Outnumbered for sure, but they must have found us intimidating because leather-legs leaned over and whispered in hair-girl's ear, after which she turned toward us, smiled, and said in a garbled but gruff voice, "Hello fellas. Drink?" Yup, it was them alright: Madame Janis and Mr. Jimi. I couldn't believe it. One of the guys in my group asked if we should "do" anything. "Naw, not right now, not unless they're dumb enough to brazenly put us to the test and light something up in front of us."

Too much heat for them, I suppose, to have cops so near to them in the lounge. They left shortly after our brief exchange. I've often thought that if we had checked them over, there would have been a few less performers at the concert that year. Imagine Woodstock without Janis Joplin and Jimi Hendrix. I guess we did the right thing, but we'll never know for sure.

A total of twelve state troopers were assigned to the narcotics squad inside the perimeter of the concert—one cop for every 40,000 kids. An almost impossible feat, and in the end, only one drug arrest was actually almost made inside the concert area. I say "almost" because as the undercover police were removing the suspect, a crowd of thousands surrounded the officers and began chanting and hollering. The bust was not worth the officers' safety so they "un-apprehended" the suspect immediately.

The Woodstock promoters had no concept of the enormity of the event beforehand. We were told to expect 20,000. The crowds swelled to more than 400,000. Some people had purchased tickets in advance, but most presumed they could purchase at the gate. When the crowds surged forward, the chain link fences surrounding the compound came tumbling down, which meant everyone entered freely. Even if we had additional backup that day, it would have been impossible to stop them, contain them, or arrest them.

Sadly, my Woodstock memory is tainted with the untimely death of one undeserving young man. There were two deaths that year, one was of his own accord—a drug overdose. It is the first boy who stepped from this life into eternity who remains fixed in my memory. He was barely sixteen and had run away from his home in New Jersey to attend the concert. By all accounts, it was his miscalculation on his second night at the concert that was fateful for him. He took some black plastic garbage bags and wrapped himself up in them for protection from the storm. Shortly thereafter, he fell asleep. A farm tractor pulling a tanker wagon ran over the young man, mistaking him for garbage. He died instantly. I met with his father and his uncle (who happened to be a lieutenant in the

New Jersey State Police Department) at the funeral home in Monticello, not far from Woodstock. It was a horribly sad ending for a young man who came with a dream to make a memory that would last his lifetime.

I served for twenty-one years with the New York State Police Department. Woodstock was clearly the wildest ride of those years. Forty years have passed, and I still remember him.

Michele Starkey is a brain aneurysm survivor who believes in living life to the fullest with her beloved husband, Keith, in the beautiful Hudson Valley of New York. Writing is an extension of her love for life and her hope to bring joy to all who read her stories. She is a contributing author to many of the Cup of Comfort anthologies published by Adams Media.

The Least Interesting Woodstock Story

(With the Oddest Epilogue)

By Jim Edwards

In 1969 I was working for a company called "India Imports of Rhode Island," that sold incense, beads, hookahs and apparel from India—and provided day jobs to most of the artists, musicians and sundry freaks of Providence. Many of us had bought tickets to Woodstock months before the concert, but few of us had wheels of our own to get there. Jagdish, the owner of IIRI agreed to let us borrow the company van on two conditions: We return the van on Sunday night, and we carry no dope.

I gave all my food, my wine, and weed to friends who drove their car in tandem with the van. We rode together all the way into Bethel, where we got separated, and I never saw them or my shit again until we got home. After the concession stands were torched on Friday night, I became dependent of the kindness of strange strangers. Which was cool; there was brown rice and water down at the Hog Farm and acres of hippies willing to turn a guy on for free, so I didn't want to split early . . . but I'd promised.

Sunday afternoon I gathered up as many of our contingent as I could find, and headed home. I remember feeling oddly bummed, which I attributed to my belief that every high has a crash. But there was more to it. I came to realize that I'd just attended an Irish wake of cosmic proportions, the beginning of the end of the whole hippie thing.

When I reached Interstate 95, I stopped to pick up two girls who were hitching home from the festival. One of them, a very beautiful young woman, sat next to me as I drove to Providence. I never said a word to her, I mean, I was bummed and she was just a kid in a fringe vest. Dropped her off at the bus station and forgot all about her.

A year later, I stepped off the ferry from Morocco in Algeciras, Spain, with a plane ticket home from Luxembourg and $10 in my pocket, then walked to the edge of town and stuck out my thumb. I'd been nine months gone, and I was figuring to deadhead fast as I could to catch a flight stateside before I was broke and hungry. I got a ride right away with a young American couple heading to . . . sweet Jesus, Luxembourg. Just when I was starting to feel lucky they pulled into a campground about 500 yards from where they picked me up. It turned out they had to wait at this camp to meet some friends who were on their way to Morocco, but since they promised me a ride straight through as soon as their friends arrived, I figured it was worth the wait.

There were two kinds of people in this campground, those on their way to Morocco, and those coming back—and you could spot the difference in a heartbeat. The kids who were going were all perky, full of gosh and golly and couldn't wait for adventure. The guys coming back were spent. Wasted. And most of them had only the clothes on their back. Every night we built a campfire, for returnees only, and shared stories of our travels. One night we had four or five new people talking about their adventures in Morocco, and I was looking at this one guy who was sitting with his wife on the other side of the fire, and I was overcome with the notion I knew him from somewhere. Then I got the flash, stood up, pointed to the guy, and asked him, "Did you dance naked with Joan Baez on the Hog Farm stage at Woodstock?"

I remembered him because, after dancing on the stage with Joan, he came over, still naked, and sat with the people I'd brought to Woodstock in the company van. He had been completely blitzed and came on hard to a fine looking woman in our group. So, to keep the conversation going, I asked if he had ever made that chick. He jumped up and all but leapt through the flames to physically shut me up before his wife realized what I was talking about. Apparently they had been married at the time.

I made a mental note to be more discreet from now on.

The Epilogue

Two years later, Jagdish hired a girl to work in the retail stores and do some modeling. We became friends and one day she confronted me with a wry smile, "You don't remember me, do you?"

It was true, I didn't recognize her. She was, of course, the young chick in the fringe vest. By 1973 we were more than friends and ventured to West Africa together to set up a garment factory. It was a sort of pilot project for Jagdish's dream of developing the entire third world. We were married in Gambia, in a big African bash in 1975. Next year it will be forty years since we first met at Woodstock, and we are still together and still in love . . . how cool is that?

Jim Edwards and Dena returned in 1978 to a post-war America slipping into disco and conservative politics. They started a family and opened their own India apparel business, which went belly up after eight years, leaving Jim, forty and never having had a straight job, to discover that the hardest part of "selling out" was trying to find a buyer. He found his niche in developing lines of high-tech golf apparel (really). Dena became a very successful toy designer, and they have two sons, one writes website code and has an indie rock band in Brooklyn; the other just released an amazing underground hip-hop CD.

The First Attempt to Land a Man on Earth

—Abbie Hoffman's view of Woodstock

By Yerucham Teitelbaum

My life found direction in 1956 when Russia launched Sputnik and American engineering schools like Cornell went from four to five-year programs to compensate. I enrolled in Cornell's electrical engineering program in 1957, where I was a straight arrow student until the summer of 1962, when I decided to drive to California. A couple of days before the trip, I had tried to find my older brother in the East Village. He wasn't at his usual Saturday night haunt, i.e., Jimmy Porter's apartment. But a frenetic folk singing guitarist named Tim Hardin was there, played a few tunes for me, and then told me he needed a ride across the country, so I told him to be ready Tuesday morning.

(Tim became the first folksinger to pick up an electric guitar and invent folk-rock. Dylan paid tribute to Hardin with his album, "John Wesley Harding." The "g" was left-handed and nobody seemed to care years later that Tim was not really the grandson of the famous outlaw.)

In 1963, I graduated as an electrical engineer, and Lockheed Missile Company near San Francisco offered a job for September. I spent the summer in Paris and Tangiers, dancing and partying, and then moved to San Francisco, where I connected with Tim Hardin's high school friends from Eugene, Oregon—musicians, poets, and actors living in San Francisco who Tim had introduced me to the year before.

The "beat" pre-hippie scene in North Beach was all of one block long at the time, and centered around Mike Ferguson and Chloe, who shared a big commune house on Noe Hill. They inspired me to further embrace lunacy, and then I inspired everybody on the scene to dance. Mike became the keyboard player for the Charlatans, the innovators of acid rock.

At the time, North Beach had one (one!) small dancing club, so small the dancing spilled out into the streets. Mike had heard about Timothy Leary experimenting with LSD in Boston, so he called him and said there's a constant party going on in San Francisco. So Timothy Leary headed west, and sometime after, Mike opened a boutique on the corner of Haight and Ashbury called For Mad Hatters Only. Millions came.

When John Fitzgerald Kennedy was assassinated, the world turned upside down. Lyndon Johnson took over. First, he cut "defense" spending by 25 percent, which meant the new hires—including me—at Lockheed were the first to be laid off, so I went home to New York. The nation re-elected LBJ as the peace candidate in 1964, and he quietly expanded the Vietnam War in 1965, eventually becoming the recipient of chants intoning his secretiveness. The most famous: Hey, hey LBJ, how many kids did you kill today?

Suddenly, television offered the masses a fairly accurate, sophisticated world-view. Graphic footage from Vietnam played on the screen nightly. Seeing "the enemy" (including Vietnamese women and children) on TV made it harder to hate them. I wrote a thesis on the history and future of communications media, based on Marshall McLuhan, the communications' theorist and father of the phrases "the medium is the message" and "global village."

By the time Martin Luther King and Robert Kennedy were assassinated in 1968, I still held down a day job, but gravitated to performing nightly as "the house dancer" at the Electric Circus, an East Village club where the hottest rock music of the time was interspersed with top-flight circus acts. One regular was the president of the Hell's Angels, who often performed a high wire act with his fellow gang members always in attendance. Another regular favorite was pantomime performer Michael Grando, a student of Marcel Marceau. Eventually, I "mimicked" his act in my dancing, as well as the karate of my "brotherly friends," i.e., the bouncers. Antonioni conducted all auditions for the 1970 anti-war movie "Zabriskie Point" at the Electric Circus. Eerily, a biplane continually flew over the outdoor scenes with "no war" painted on one wing and "no words" on the other.

Of course I went to Woodstock.

At Woodstock, the torrential rains of Friday night had given way to searing heat on Saturday. A vendor tried to overcharge for water and was quickly relieved of his supplies. As Charlie Chin and the All-Night Newsboys put it in an Electric Circus favorite, "The street giveth and the street taketh away."

Then it rained again. On Sunday, the torrential rains stopped, but the concert didn't continue right away. Gathered around bonfires to keep warm and to dry out, the audience spontaneously created the "rain chant." Symbolic of power going to the people, David Peel and the Lower East Side band led us in "Ahhhahahaaaahhha, no rain, no rain, no rain . . . " and the Woodstock Nation created its own music, and really got into it.

I had not bought a ticket, but a year later the promoters and producers of Woodstock made their money back on me. I saw the movie on the big screen every day for a week, chiefly to watch my five seconds of immortality—banging a beer bottle with a stick during the rain chant.

Yerucham Teitelbaum, the first hippie on earth, has secretly co-directed world events for half a century. Among other innovations, he was the original kid for Mr. Wizard, invented break-dancing, real-time computer processing, and thought of the Internet first. He embraced organic food in 1970 and ran a macrobiotic house in Brooklyn Heights, while camping on weekends in the real town of Woodstock, before moving to a farm in Ulster County, New York. These days, besides growing Indian corn, he writes high-tech patents and lives with his wife and kids in the Negev Desert.

My Dad Made Me Do it

By Anita Lopez Winder

I bounced onto the field at Woodstock on Wednesday afternoon in the back seat of a vintage 1959 turnpike cruiser with very bad shocks. My friend Suze and I had decided to team up and hitchhike to Bethel. We had graduated from high school in June; I was college bound in September, and Suze, well, Suze was just Suze.

Suze banged on the screen door at my folks house right on time on Wednesday morning. After a quick inventory we were happy to find that we had $40 between us, and some pot. Luck was with us, and after two rides that took us off Aquidneck Island, we were happily thumbing a ride on a westbound ramp of the Massachusetts Turnpike headed to New York. When the cruiser and its three occupants pulled over, the party, as they say, began. We tuned in, dropped out, and turned on with a boda bag of cheap wine and joints rolled in papers that were aptly colored red, white, and blue.

My dad was a friend of Mr. Wein, who produced the Newport Jazz and Folk Festivals. Dad was treated to free tickets each year, and in 1963, he took me along to hear my first live music. I was twelve years old and awestruck. As the parade of performers crossed the stage, Dad provided fascinating running commentary. My musical education had begun.

Later that summer, Dad gave me fifty cents and dropped me off at the gates of a folk music workshop at the Newport Folk Festival. I paid my admission and was thrilled at being left on my own for a few hours. Pete Seeger, Bob Dylan, and others sang their songs. As I looked around at the audience, it hit me like a thunderbolt: I was one of them. I fit in perfectly with the music and the politics of it all. My lifelong love of music had begun.

My parents were music buffs, Democrats, and blue collar. Left wing politics of the 1960s shaped my anti-war stance concerning the Vietnam War, but I was a lazy protester at best. I was a music junkie first and foremost. By the time I bounced into Bethel, I realized that I had been given the gift of a very good ear for music.

We bounced along the road at the top of the hill. Looking to the right, we saw a big stage at the field's bottom. We stopped the cruiser about half way down the slope and Suze and I walked down to the stage that was being hammered together. We were soon invited to hop aboard a flatbed truck packed with hippies headed to town on a beer run, and then on to the local waterfalls for a swim. Those with guitars played, and we sang our way through the country lanes. We passed cows in the neighboring fields and a few farmers on their tractors, most of whom waved a hello with their caps. It was a most perfect evening.

Thursday flew by as I soon lost track of Suze, the cruiser, and its occupants. I had dropped a hit of acid early in the morning and spent the day swimming in the ponds near the field and hanging around the various campfires. Scores of hippies were obviously enjoying the freedom. Even before the music started, the greatest rumor of all was making its way around the field: Jimi himself was going to play.

As dawn broke on Friday morning, I chose my spot in front of the stage about 50 feet back and dead center. I made friends with those around me and a mini camp of sorts was soon established. It was about that time that the most astonishing thing about Woodstock (other than the music) began—a constant flow of beer, wine, boda bags, pot, pipes, fruit, hats, water, blankets, acid, kazoos, drums, love beads, flags, and even fully cooked hamburgers on buns with mustard and onions. Boxes and boxes of these things passed through the crowd. Take what you needed, throw something in. The Diggers, otherwise known as members of the Hog Farm commune, came through the crowd handing out hot oatmeal and a flower for your hair. It was a slice of heaven, and I danced and clapped all day, every day.

At Woodstock pot, hash, and acid was everywhere. I did see some other harder drugs around, but I was never interested in any of that. I was into smoking joints and hash and dropping some of the good acid that was being passed around by the bagfull.

The scene at Woodstock was just what you see in the movie footage. If you think it looked like fun, and if you think the music was great, then multiply that by a billion. And yes, I waited it out through the downpours to Monday morning to see Jimi play.

Forty years later, I can still remember traversing the back roads on the flat bed truck singing along with the others in the evening light and waving back at the farmers as they raised their caps to us. And how could I ever forget the thrill of seeing Richie Havens, Janis Joplin, The Grateful Dead, Santana, and Crosby, Stills, Nash & Young? I bet I am the only person who can really say, in all truth, "I went to Woodstock, and my dad made me do it."

Thanks, Dad!

Anita Lopez Winder happily survived the 1960s and now lives in northern Florida.

She travels all over the United States and overseas to hear music of many genres with like-minded friends. She continues to enjoy a gifted and music-filled life and plans on returning to Bethel for the 40th anniversary of Woodstock.

Sojourn '69

By Scott A. Munroe

In 1965, at age thirteen, on a trip to California to visit my uncle, we did something that changed this small-town Pennsylvania boy forever—we drove down Sunset Boulevard, where observing the hippies hanging out at Pandora's Box blew my mind. Despite Beatle haircuts, boys with long hair were often ridiculed and rarely seen in my area. The bell-bottom ways of the hippies on Sunset Boulevard awakened a Bohemian spirit that sparked the creative artist in me. Back home, my high school art teacher introduced me to Andy Warhol and Dali, which further facilitated a leap into the psychedelic scene. Soon, my musical tastes began to change: The Animals, Barry McGuire, and The Byrds replaced The Beach Boys, Jan and Dean, and Chubby Checker. No more twisting for this American boy.

My next awakening occurred in 1967 during the legendary Summer of Love. The Doors rocking Light My Fire; The Beatles smoking Sergeant Pepper; and Jimi Hendrix killing Are You Experienced? had me rushing down to the local record store the days their albums arrived. I still have many of them, scratched from thousands of plays. I was traveling to the beat of my own (way cool) drum.

In 1968, I could drive, which launched phase four of my transformation. The Electric Factory (nightclub) opened, and WMMR FM (radio) launched "The Marconi Experiment," a pioneering underground program that played our music instead of our parents' music, both of which enticed my friends and I to drive to Philly to see the bands we loved— live. On Sunday November 17, 1968, Jefferson Airplane appeared at the Factory with Headlights, offering a spectacular concert and light show. The Philly Spectrum hosted the first Quaker City Rock Festival that year, featuring The Chambers Brothers, Big Brother and the Holding Co., with Janis Joplin, Vanilla Fudge, Moby Grape, and the Buddy Guy Blues Band. Meanwhile, WMMR played all the cool songs from 9 P.M. to 6 A.M., and that's where I first heard about the Atlantic City Pop Festival and Woodstock.

I had just graduated in 1969, was headed to art school in the fall, and had taken a job in a print shop, printing labels for bottles. I was also a roadie for a friend's band, and had helped them paint their 1950s delivery truck to resemble the Cream's Wheels of Fire LP cover, and then added assorted psychedelic designs. Boy did we blow some minds when we drove it to school for the art teacher to grade. Of course we all got A's.

The Atlantic City concert was cool, and I overheard so much buzz about Woodstock, I was determined to go. Unfortunately, the guys in the band couldn't go, so I prepared to hitchhike. Luckily, a co-worker (Tom) at the print shop said that he and his girlfriend were going. None of us had tickets.

When traffic no longer inched forward, Tom pulled into a field and told me to head over to the concert site right away, saying they would set up camp and join me later. I knew the likelihood that I would see them again was nil . . . still, I was itching to get on with it, and thus quickly joined the exodus of humanity. I was seventeen and on my own in that giant crowd—and I loved it. After all, I was a grizzled concert veteran and no stranger to the lysergic acid diethylamide experience. I didn't feel paranoid in big crowds; besides there were so many beautiful hippie chicks to check out. I might get lucky (I didn't).

Even though a police officer sat nearby in his patrol car, dealers holding signs saying "hash, pot, or acid" openly hawked their "goodies." Campsites filled the woods on either side of the road, but it was what I saw when I reached the concert site that blew me away—Whoa! I was astounded. The hillside was already jam-packed so I settled about three-quarters of the way up the hill from the stage, to the right of center, where a couple shared their blanket with me for three days.

The place was buzzing. You could feel a collective connection, and a sense early on that we were making history. I had come for the music and saw everyone I wanted to see, with the exception of Jimi Hendrix. My fondest memories, yes I remember, occurred at twilight when lights and campfires glowed as far as you could see. The phenomenal voice of Joan Baez singing We Shall Overcome moved me to tears—of joy. The crispness of all the fantastic lead guitars, and the thump of the bass guitars in that fresh country air were fantastic. Janis! "Wanna take you higher! Higher! Higher!" Sly! "Good morning people!" Grace Slick and the Airplane playing while the sun rose in the background! Goin' Home Ten Years After! Also, of course—"Gimme an F!"

Just before dawn on Monday, I walked slowly back towards the campsite, praying I would find Tom still parked in that field. I did—they had never left the campsite. I nibbled on the food they offered, and then crashed in the back seat, sleeping almost the entire way home.

All my friends wanted the low-down, which made me feel like a celebrity for a few days. But I focused on art school in Pittsburgh and worried about the possibility of being drafted. I lucked out again—I was never called into active service.

I drove up to see the Bethel Woods Center for the Arts that opened recently as a testament to the Woodstock Music & Art Festival that put that area of upstate New York on the map. The fields lay silent now, and frankly it's hard to recreate in my mind what occurred, but here's the important part: It happened, and I was there. So I stood there, on what will forever be Max Yasgur's farm to me, silently inhaling a little of the essence of those three glorious days in that psychedelic summer of 1969.

Scott Munroe is an artist living in Reading, Pennsylvania. He also breeds bulldogs and works in a racecar fabrication shop. Scott is happily married, the father of three daughters, and grandfather to three.

A Spiritual Journey: Meeting the Woodstock Guru

By Rev. Prem Anjali, PhD

The journey of a thousand miles begins with a single step.

—Lao-tzu

Age sixteen, clutching my ticket, I began hitchhiking to the Woodstock festival. Soon overcome with concern about how much trouble I would get into when my parents found out, and a rising realization that I'd never been far from home and how risky this could be, this small-town Jersey girl put her thumb down and went home. Little did I realize that the journey of a thousand miles had already begun . . .

Who would have guessed then that ten years later I would meet and become the personal assistant to Swami Satchidananda, also known as Swamiji to his followers and the "Woodstock Guru" to many?

Swamiji himself told me that the promoters had expected a large crowd but, as hundreds of thousands poured into the farm, they became concerned. One of the people in charge had met Swamiji and felt that his calming vibration could have a soothing effect on the crowd, so the organizers asked him to come immediately.

Victor Zurbel described to me how he and some other students jammed into a car and drove Swamiji from New York City toward Woodstock. As soon as they exited the freeway, the roads were so crowded with cars and people, a police escort was summoned to drive Swamiji to the site. Along the way, when a teenage boy fell off the back of a car, Swamiji insisted on stopping so he could sit beside him, rubbing his head gently and soothingly, until help arrived. When the roads became too clogged, even for the police, a special helicopter was pressed into service.

Steve (now known as "Muruga") Booker, the drummer for Tim Hardin, was one of several musicians also waiting for the helicopter. When I met Muruga years later, he described looking up and seeing this man with a long beard, in flowing orange robes approach and feeling right away that Swamiji was the most spiritual being he'd ever seen. Muruga had dabbled in meditation and was deeply searching to find himself. He began softly playing his clay drums, hoping Swamiji would notice and say something to him, but just then the helicopter came and carried Swamiji to the site.

When the helicopter touched down, the organizers ran to meet it and were so happy to see Swamiji, they gathered around him, some holding microphones hoping to interview him before leading him to the backstage area. The helicopter flew back to pick up Muruga and the other musicians. Muruga described flying over the site, looking down on a massive area that looked as if it were covered with swarming ants. When they landed and Muruga went backstage, Swamiji pointed to him and said, "There's that American boy I mentioned who plays the drum like the tabla players in India."

Seeing an opening, Muruga approached Swamiji, played his drums again, and then asked, "Swami, what is life about?"

According to Muruga, Swami Satchidananda pointed to the audience and explained, "They are energy. You are energy, and all of you musicians who have gathered here are energy too. This energy of the audience has come to see the energy of all the different bands. When you go out on stage, if you are positive, you can help direct the energy of the audience to go positive. If you are negative, you could help them to go negative. The choice is yours, and life is energy with a choice of going positive or negative."

Swamiji then told Muruga to come and see him at the Integral Yoga Institute in New York. Suddenly a light bulb went off in Muruga's head. He told me, "I realized he was Peter Max's guru." In the 1960s Peter Max had painted many pop art pictures with Swamiji as the subject. After Woodstock, I went to see him and became his disciple. If not for Woodstock, I would never have gotten into yoga and received Swamiji's guidance, which further transformed everything else in my life.

Again, I wasn't at Woodstock, but I've listened to Swami Satchidananda's filmed opening remarks many times, and offer this excerpt:

"My beloved sisters and brothers, I am overwhelmed with joy to see the youth of America gathered here in the name of the fine art of music. In fact, through music we can work wonders. . . One thing I very much wish you all to remember: with sound we can make or break. On certain battlefields animal sounds are used. Without such sounds—war cries—human beings couldn't become the kind of animals that kill their own brethren. So I am very happy to see that we are all gathered to create some 'making' sounds rather than 'breaking' sounds, to find that peace and joy through the celestial music. I am honored for having been given the opportunity of opening this great, great music festival.

"America leads the world in several ways. Very recently, when I was in the East, the grandson of Mahatma Gandhi asked me, 'What's happening in America?' I said, 'America is becoming a whole. America is helping everybody in the material field, but the time has come for America to help the whole world with spirituality also.'

"That's why across its length and breadth, we see people, thousands and thousands of people, yoga-minded, spiritual-minded. So let all our actions and all our arts express yoga or unity. Through the sacred art of music let us find peace that will pervade all over the globe. Often people shout, 'We are going to fight for peace!' I still do not understand how they are going to fight and then find peace. Therefore, let us not fight for peace, but let us find peace within ourselves first.

"The future of the whole world is in your hands. You can make it or break it. But you are really here to make the world and not to break it. There is a dynamic manpower here. Hearts are meeting . . .

"I, with all my heart, wish a great, great success to this music festival. Let it pave the way for many more festivals in other parts of the country . . . The entire world is going to know what the American youth can do for humanity. Every one of you should feel responsibility for the outcome of this festival. Once again, let me express my sincere wish and prayers for the success and peace of this celebration. Thank you. OM Shanthi Shanthi Shanthi."

Rev. Prem Anjali, PhD had the good fortune to travel the globe as assistant to Sri Swami Satchidananda for twenty-five years. She is the editor of the quarterly journal, Integral Yoga Magazine. She is also the editor of two biographies about Swami Satchidananda and she produced the film, Living Yoga: The Life and Teachings of Swami Satchidananda, which is available on DVD.

Where to Now, Pilgrim?

By Robert Paul Blumenstein

The 1962 Studebaker, when it pulled into my driveway on August 13, 1969, had dings along the side panels and rust spreading across the bumper. Nevertheless, that was the car that my friend Moby swore would take us from Greenville, South Carolina, to the town of Bethel, New York, and maybe back.

I had rolled up my sleeping bag, filled my backpack with dry clothes, toiletries, and a few cans of food. We planned to stop on the road and finish gathering provisions for our pilgrimage to that sacred patch of terra firma, where the world would see that peace and love had now become a way of life. That's how Moby and his front seat passenger Levi and I saw it.

Unfortunately, that's not how my father saw it. For him, it was a different matter altogether. He stopped me at the door and said in a steady voice, "If you leave, don't ever come back here again."

Universally speaking, teenagers and conundrums are wedded partners. They're always faced with the prospect of choosing one path or the other, no matter how sharply or subtlety they diverge: drink that beer, or just say no thank you; have sex, or wait until marriage; smoke that weed, or don't inhale. At that time in my life, like all teenagers, I faced the same riddle: What happens if I do, or, what will happen if I don't?

I opposed the Vietnam War with effusive passion. Yet, it was more than the issues germane to Southeast Asia that fueled my fire against this war; my dad bought a portable television and set the thing on the end of the dining table. We sat at our table night-after-night watching soldiers and innocent victims die and babies burn. Even as a teenager, I saw nothing sensible, heroic, or justifiable in the devastation that takes place in war.

Also, the very same summer of Woodstock, the dude across the street returned home from a tour of duty in Vietnam. His parents had sewn several bed sheets together and painted on the words "Welcome home, Harvey!" (similar to the yellow ribbon thing that came later) and planted the banner in their front yard. I'll never forget the day Harvey showed up. Within the first hour of his arrival, he marched out into the front yard and ripped the banner down.

A different set of values was on the line when my dad stepped in front of me and said, "You leave, you don't come back." In less than two weeks, I would start my senior year in high school—my last year before attaining commencement of adulthood—so I made what I thought was an adult decision.

Moby backed his Studebaker out of our driveway and Levi never got the chance to argue with me over who got the front seat. I found out later that Chipper, the fourth pilgrim of our sojourn, had been given the same ultimatum by his mother that my father had given me. And so it turned out that only Moby and Levi made it to Woodstock. Other pilgrims from Greenville boasted that they went to Woodstock, but, "couldn't get in," something about being stuck on the freeway.

So, after Levi returned home I asked him how it was.

Levi answered, "Heavy, man."

"Yeah? How so?"

"It was just, heavy, man."

I didn't want to ask him a silly, clichéd question as to whether Woodstock had altered the earth's gravitational field, so I let it go and then asked Moby the same question.

"Wow, far out. I've never seen so many damn people crammed into one place in my life. We couldn't even get to the stage and we got there a little more than a day early. Just the mass of humanity was mind blowing."

I didn't let up because at least Moby was forking over some details. I asked more questions about the bands, their campsite, did they have enough food to eat, could they leave and come back, and a few other really dumb questions. I was astounded when Moby said, "Man, all I did was drop acid for three days and trip my brains out. I really don't remember much of anything."

Since then, I have met other Woodstock pilgrims that have shared similar accounts. Each time I hear an account like Moby's I wonder, what did I miss? And I wonder, too, if I have held so fastidiously onto a dream of peace and love, that I might have only done so because I didn't go to Woodstock. Maybe the trip to Woodstock wasn't all in my mind like my acid-dropping friends experienced; maybe it was all in my heart. As I watch our country continue to perfect the machines of war and beat the drum for warriors to gather, and silence voices like mine with clever little media sayings like, "oppose the war, not the warrior," I wonder where will we go from here, pilgrims? Will we ever be able to say, after that grand day in the sun at Woodstock, "no more soldiers, no more wars?"

Robert Paul Blumenstein resides in Midlothian, Virginia, with his wife, Ann, and miniature schnauzer, Fitzgerald. He writes full time and is a member of the Earl Hamner Theater playwrights' conference in Nelson County, Virginia, where he is an actor and opinion voicer. Check out his latest novel Snapping the String and other published work at www.robertblumenstein.com.

Finding My Way Home

By Vinny Stefanelli

I was fifteen, living in a broken home in Erie, Penn., and obsessed with music. I had been studying guitar for seven years, and if I wasn't playing my guitar, I was reading about music. I found out about Woodstock either in Rolling Stone or the Village Voice. I tore out the advertisement listing all of the bands that would be appearing—an astounding number of great bands—and showed it to my brother (who was twenty) in hopes he would provide a ride. He glanced at the ad, put it in his pocket, and that seemed to be the end of it.

I had given up on going when he came to me weeks later and nonchalantly said that one of his friends couldn't go to the concert and asked if I wanted to go. At first, I was pissed off that he had been planning to go without me . . . but I was also ecstatic, so I surrendered the anger immediately and said "hell yeah!"

A week later, five of us hopped into a car and drove six hours to reach Woodstock, and what turned out to be the greatest experience a fifteen-year-old boy could ever have. I had no expectations, other than to see and hear musicians I idolized; but I truly had no idea the music would actually be secondary to the spiritual experience.

We arrived late afternoon and found a space to ditch the car before heading to the concert. We walked in total darkness following the sounds in the distance. Even now, forty years later, it's hard to describe, or even explain, the euphoria I felt. As we neared the area, the music, as well as the smell of reefer and cow manure grew more intense, but to me, it all felt truly magical. As we came up over the hill, the sight of the stage and the sea of people was overwhelming. I had never seen so many people.

When my foot struck what appeared to be a rock, I looked down and realized I had stepped on some guy's head. My victim took my hand, shook it, and said: "Don't worry man, it's cool." And suddenly I knew that I was in a safe place—I was home.

We listened to music until we got tired, and then walked back to the car, where we slept wherever we could find a comfortable spot. People milled around everywhere, but it was so dark, I couldn't see anyone, so I just listened. I heard people laughing, talking, singing, and making love, yet I remember, oddly, feeling a deep sense of loneliness, and at the same time a deep connectedness, as if my spirit was literally expanding. The feeling of loneliness disappeared when I fell asleep, but the expansion of spirit remained.

The next day, we headed back to the concert site early so we could score a place close to the stage. Some people were leaving, so we made our way to the stage and claimed a spot on the ground where we would plant ourselves for the next twenty hours, leaving only once to search for food—and only after unrolling our sleeping bags to save our space.

We walked until we found what appeared to be the only store in the entire area. The shelves were bare, but fellow concertgoers circled them repeatedly, as if they expected the shelves to be restocked any minute. And thus we returned empty-handed, and very hungry, but not long thereafter what I called the miracle of the loaves and fish occurred— suddenly food appeared. Mostly, we received bites of granola, dried fruit, and crackers, but it all tasted great. And for the rest of the day, something was passed along continuously, including some great weed.

The music eventually began and even though we experienced downpours and rain delays, even though the towers occasionally swayed dangerously in the wind, and even though I didn't visit a rest room for nearly two days, it was a glorious experience. I saw and heard Richie Havens, Country Joe McDonald, John Sebastian, Santana, Mountain, Creedence Clearwater Revival, Sly and the Family Stone, Jefferson Airplane, Joe Cocker, Country Joe and the Fish, Ten Years After, The Band, Johnny Winter, Blood, Sweat and Tears, Crosby, Stills, Nash & Young, Sha-Na-Na . . . and in-between one set, I stared into Joan Baez's blue eyes, and she smiled at me.

Around 4 A.M. Monday, my brother and his friends decided it was time to leave. I was so mesmerized by the sounds of CSN&Y I wasn't about to leave this event, this experience. I felt totally at home, and I had come to see my guitar hero, Jimi Hendrix, who had yet to take the stage. So, without thinking, I nonchalantly turned to my brother and said, "Go ahead. I'll be home in a couple of days." Unfortunately he was the older brother who had brought me and who felt responsible for my safety, so he and his friends grabbed me by the shirt and physically escorted me out.

On the long, tiring, and boring ride home, I realized that I was returning home a different person, one who could never again conform to traditional expectations. And here's the best part, forty years later, some of the memories have faded, but that expansion of spirit I first experienced at Woodstock still remains strong.

Vinny Stefanelli began his career as a professional musician at the age of fifteen. He is an accomplished guitarist and media producer who has worked for the past thirty-five years in the music, film, and game industries. After living for ten years in New York City and ten years in the San Francisco Bay area, he returned to his hometown of Erie, Pennsylvania, where he lives with his wife and two daughters.

Lost Innocence

By Robert Rohloff

At the age of fifty-eight I still think about the sixties, and the counterculture generation that questioned the direction of American society. For some, the revolution was all about drugs, love, flowers, and beads. For me, it was all about lost innocence. In 1969, my life changed forever.

I grew up in a small town in Nebraska where sports were more important than an education and rednecks were a dime a dozen. In 1968, my school expelled me for refusing to get a crew cut. My friends abandoned me when I grew my hair long and started listening to what they considered drug tunes. I couldn't go anywhere without being fearful of being beaten up or killed. I was often chased home by drunken rednecks threatening to cut my hair.

In June 1969, I used drugs for the first time at the Denver Pop Festival at Mile High Stadium in Colorado. I hitchhiked there to see my favorite band, The Jimi Hendrix Experience. At the festival, I met some hippies who lived on a communal farm in upstate New York, who offered me some LSD called Purple Haze. The acid made the music dance circles inside my head, like a circus playing in my mind. It was the first time I tried LSD, and the first time I heard about Woodstock.

Before leaving Denver, I exchanged phone numbers with Paul, one of the hippies. He said I could crash at their farm and go along with them to the event, if I liked. He then handed me a bag of pills, which I took home and stashed them beneath my mattress.

August 8, 1969 my plans of going to Woodstock crashed in flames. As a teenager approaching age eighteen, I found out that the fist draft lottery would be held in December. I felt too heartsick to even think about Woodstock, and that little bag of pills stashed under my mattress kept me high for a week—and depressed, so depressed I didn't care if I lived or died.

On August 18, 1969, around 11 P.M., Paul called, babbling about mushrooms, a falling fence, a free concert, traffic jams, freaks playing in the mud, and some far out hash. He told me in great detail how the music had blown his mind. How Janis Joplin was so high she could hardly stand straight, and that the Grateful Dead, Canned Heat, and Santana were all incredible. He told me about how when they introduced Hendrix as The Jimi Hendrix Experience, Hendrix corrected them and said the new name of his band was Gypsy Sun and Rainbows. Listening to Paul I finally felt 'in tune' with my generation, outside small-town Nebraska anyway.

December 1, 1969, the day of the draft lottery, my birth date drew number eighty. When the TV announcer said, "If you're in the top 100, you will be called to serve in Vietnam," I rushed to the bathroom, threw up, retreated to my room, and cried. My childhood innocence vanished within seconds.

Sometime that summer, I received the dreaded letter from the draft board, informing me to report for military duty in September. On September 15, 1970, high on marijuana, I stood alongside a North Dakota highway, in a drizzly rain—my Gibson guitar wrapped in plastic—trying to thumb a ride to Canada. When I had told my father and mother I was going to Canada instead of going off to war, Mom called me "a yellowbelly." Father said I should do what I thought right, and then I saw something for the first time in my life—I saw Father cry.

Over the last thirty-five years I have seen a lot of great bands at different festivals. I still attend as many peace marches as I can, and always try to spread the message of peace and love. Memories of how Paul had described the Woodstock festival make me feel good inside and remember the most important thing I took out of the sixties—to be able to enjoy the small things life has to offer. You could say that skinny, pimply faced kid that left the States in 1970 because of his beliefs, grew up to be a man that could deal with the world around him—without drugs—and still able to play in the mud.

Robert Rohloff hitchhiked across Canada and most of the United States as a young man, and credits that experience with his knowledge of human nature. He is a collector of exotic daggers and musical instruments. He comes from Bohemian ancestry, and that accounts for his gypsy soul and his bohemia way of life. Website: www.yonisha.com/rohloff.html

One Flakey Chick at Yasgur's Farm

By Barbara L. Heller

During the summer of '69, I was a nineteen-year-old returning college student at SUNY New Paltz, following a calamitous second semester when I literally turned on, crashed in a public speaking class, and dropped out. After going back home to live with my folks on Long Island and working in a supermarket for a few months, I signed up to attend summer classes.

The late '60s were a time of "in-betweens" for me, and my generation. I took on a new identity—I changed my name, let my bleached hair grow out, and experimented with drugs, sex, and rock 'n roll. While I organized anti-war teach-ins, a former high school boyfriend enlisted in the Marines. Sorrowful assassinations had already occurred—JFK, MLK, RFK, Malcolm X—but the violence of Kent State and the brutal assault of my college roommate had not. The first waves of the feminist resurgence were evident, but women's studies classes hadn't yet begun. Male politicos still assumed we "girls" would get the coffee and take notes at SDS meetings.

That summer an acquaintance mentioned that the organizers of an upstate music festival were looking for workers for the weekend. Mid-week I hitched with him upstate to a Yasgur's farm, where we sat for hours on a hill in the hot sun waiting for our three-minute interviews. I emerged from the official trailer with a job offer for evening shifts at the Food for Love booths.

The Hog Farm, a hippie-commune group, was organizing a large camp out, so my new friend and I decided to stay to help with preparations. People were sharing places to sleep, things to smoke, food to eat (rice and beans and odd assortments of veggies), and there were small jam sessions and, at this early part of the festivities, accessible toilets. We bathed and went skinny-dipping in a nearby lake, which was a tad intimate, like squeezing into a hot tub that's just a little too small with a bunch of your friends.

My then-current boyfriend, Charlie (he later became my ex-husband), wouldn't come to Bethel earlier in the week; a temperamental student-artist, he didn't want to miss studio time. So when another friend said he was driving back to New Paltz to pick up friends, I went hoping to convince Charlie to come along.

Friday afternoon Charlie accompanied me back to Yasgur's Farm. The small ripple of pre-concert crowds had turned into magnificent waves of tsunami proportions. There were hundreds, thousands, and hundreds of thousands more carefree and colorful characters walking the path. Our driver supposedly knew a shortcut, but we still had to park a couple of miles from the entrance. I ran to get to work on time, and my stand was already full of workers and running out of sandwiches (the weekend's food ran out before my shift ended). Food buyers and sellers were equally enveloped in the mood and music; we all sang and danced as we served and ate.

Later that night, Charlie and I stumbled around in the dark to find the tent I had stayed in for the pre-concert period. The area had been extended with tarps and haphazardly hung blankets and looked like a refuge camp. Bodies were separate, hinged, and piled with no room to fit any more. One guy shouted out, "There's room . . . but only for chicks."

We continued our search and ended up under a trailer hoisted up on cinder blocks. The next morning I awoke to a gentle touch on my shoulder and a whisper, "You two have to come out from there. The trailer is beginning to tilt from all the rain, and we think it might fall." We emerged, faces half masked with mud, just as Grace Slick, from center stage, announced, "It's a brand new day."

When it was time to leave, Charlie and I joined a slow line of cars, many of us sitting on the front hoods singing. Some locals sold glasses of water for a dollar to those in our thirsty horde who had cash. Others seemed cautious, curious, yet concerned, like the woman who offered me a glass of ice tea and the use of her bathroom—both of which I gratefully accepted.

When I returned to school I had missed almost a week of a six-week English class. I pleaded with my professor, who reluctantly agreed to give me an extension even though I attributed my absence to "astrological problems."

At Woodstock, we were suspended in time. We didn't know we were making history; we were just having fun, taking a break. Unlike the peace marches—where we were vigilant and self-righteous, trying to feel strong and effective yet often feeling powerless to change our own lives, let alone the direction of the country—at Woodstock, we felt vital and strong, unconcerned and unselfconscious. We didn't know how lucky we were.

Barbara L Heller is a clinical social worker who has been in private practice as a psychotherapist for over a quarter of a century. She is also the author of 365 Ways to Relax Mind, Body, and Soul and How To Sleep Soundly Tonight. Currently on sabbatical, you can read her travelogue at www.thedreamyear.blogspot.com.

Ribbon of Humanity

By Valerie Ptak LaMont

We were three girls in a tidal wave of fellow hippies: me, my summer roommate Terry, and Mary, who planned to meet up with her boyfriend, Joe. My friend Roy had left early to pick up his girlfriend and said he'd join us later. Little did we know just how improbable meetings would become as we became part of the joyous ribbon of humanity that wound its way to the Woodstock Music & Art Fair.

As we walked along in jubilation we could hear the buzz—the Thruway was closed and the festival was free, open to anyone who could get there. We could hear Richie Havens even before we got there and saw the vast crowd ahead of us. How could Roy find us in this, and how could we find Joe?

Amazingly, we found Joe despite the crush, along with his little brother, and settled in to enjoy folk artists like Melanie and Tim Hardin. When the rains came, much of the crowd retreated to the shelter of their tents. Our tent was with Roy—wherever he was—so we opted to get as close to the stage as possible and moved up between the two towers. The view of the stage was perfect, and, as the rains ceased, I was so close to Joan Baez and Arlo Guthrie I was in folkie heaven.

The next morning, the first sight that greeted us was a naked man enjoying the dawn. Feeling that this was a bit much for his little brother, Joe decided to go. No way could we leave this. Even Mary chose to stay, but that made it more imperative than ever to find Roy. We had no food, but I'd brought uppers, and they sustained us by keeping away the hunger.

I trooped all over Yasgur's farm, from the pond to the woods and back to the music. I watched people bathing naked and hippies dancing in the woods. Saturday evolved into a day of celebration despite the mud and the uncertainty of our situation. Unfamiliar, exciting music had people slip-sliding in the mud to its strains. Someone said it was a group named Santana electrifying the crowd.

Finally, from a bank of pay phones, I got through to Roy. Unable to get to the festival, he'd driven to Buffalo, stranding us. As I walked back to tell the girls, local farmers were selling milk from the back of their trucks. One quart was put in my hand with instructions to take some and pass it on. We didn't know each other, but we were all in this together, caught up in our spirit of community. We didn't have a way home, but we had new friends, music, and, at times, sunshine.

Reality hit us on Sunday when the rain interrupted Joe Cocker. By late afternoon we knew we'd have no chance to dry out. The uppers were gone, and Terry and Mary were coming down. We abandoned our sodden sleeping bags and slogged our way out of Woodstock Nation to the nearby town of Bethel. Luckily, the Woodstock experience had extended outside the festival boundaries. The people at the first house we came to invited us in like we were family. They gave us a piece of cardboard and pens so we could make a sign for hitchhiking and fed us turkey soup. As we took our position by the roadside, holding our sign, we saw a boy hitching opposite us who was shirtless. A local motorist stopped, took off his own shirt and gave it to the boy.

A boy from Syracuse picked us up, and then stopped for others. By the time we left Bethel, the car held seven of us. Somewhere north of Binghamton the car broke down. Realizing that no one would stop for seven hitchers, I called my parents—in the middle of the night—and my dad drove two hours to rescue us and our Good Samaritan. We all crashed at my parents' house, where we watched my mom burn my dress because it smelled so bad.

The next year was a volatile one for colleges. We had police on our campus in February. Kent State hit us hard. Always politically active, I took to the streets to protest the invasion of Cambodia. I manned a makeshift infirmary to help kids who'd been tear-gassed. We were all together in the "mud" of forging a better world. Because of Woodstock I knew that if we worked together we could accomplish anything.

Woodstock also taught me not to judge people by labels; the locals were just as generous as the hippies. I took home no souvenirs, but feelings of peace and love stayed with me. Today I work in a library at a major university. I greet each new freshman as a member of my community. I have had students interview me on my Woodstock experiences. Most of all, I try to get them to think beyond themselves, to participate in the ribbon of humanity—and to vote. One voice can seldom be heard, but joined with others, as at Woodstock, it can change the world.

Valerie Ptak LaMont lives in rural Pennsylvania with her husband of thirty-five years. They have two grown sons, three cats and one very spoiled dog. She has edited ten books for the best selling author Sharon Kay Penman and keeps in touch with her inner college student by working at the library at the University of Pittsburgh at Titusville.

I'm in the Movie, Man

By Peter McAlevey

Woodstock succeeded on such a massive level thanks to the 1960s version of "viral marketing." We didn't have cell phones, text messaging, or the Internet, but word got around. I, along with my friends Billy Levy, Frank Colin, and Bob Gioia, dug the music scene, and, like most scenesters in that era, we were all broke. So we spent a lot of time hitchhiking (the only way to get anywhere if you had no money).

Usually, the people that picked us up were like-minded hippies traveling around in multi-colored Volkswagen vans or Bugs. Occasionally, the straight twenty-something college student picked us up, and we always liked to impress the hippies and enlighten the straight arrows, so sometime in June 1969, we began proselytizing to everyone who picked us up about this August fair in upstate New York. Hey, didja know that The Who, Jefferson Airplane, Joplin, Hendrix, et al., will be playing in the same place—for free? Well, how could you beat it?

We lived in Rockland County, a county or two south of Woodstock, or even Bethel, where the festival ended up, but flush on Route 17B, the direct route to the festival. Thus, particularly as the time grew close, we encountered many potential festival-goers. I have no idea how many people we convinced to join us there, but since just about everyone else we knew was also spreading the word, we took partial credit for the turnout. Unfortunately, we forgot to tell the organizers that, well, we were telling everyone it was free . . . but hey, what the heck, it was all in the spirit of the revolution, right?

Finally the weekend was upon us. By Friday afternoon, Frank, Billy, and Bob split to make the scene, but since I never liked lines or crowds or rain, I hung back. Anyway, after I began hearing about the traffic jams and mess on the highways, I realized two things: (1) The concert was going to be a huge party and (2) My motorcycle provided unlimited access. On it, I could always cut up between lanes or zip down country paths to get where I wanted to go.

So I hopped on the Yamaha and sped 60 miles from Suffern to Bethel. When I hit the logjam on Route 17B, being on my Yamaha saved me from going VC (Viet Cong) in all that gnarly traffic. Instead, I felt smug and empowered, like a cavalry scout on horseback, able to get where I needed to go—in a hurry. I arrived sometime in the late afternoon, and when I discovered that the fences were already down, I thought, Cool, we had correctly predicted a free concert!

Keeping an eye out for the guys, I muscled my way down the natural grass bowl to the front of the stage, and although I never found them, Frank says you can see me in the Woodstock movie, during Richie Havens's performance, straining my neck in all directions, looking around for my buddies.

I remember staying as late as Melanie's performance, when it started to rain. Then, not wanting to get drenched, I made my way back to place where I had hidden my motorcycle—in the woods, locked to a tree. Peace and happiness only went so far in those days, in my experience.

I rode back the next day in sunshine, but by then the full effect of the ecological disaster was taking effect. Forget no fences, the johns were overwhelmed and smelled ghastly, and people were relieving themselves where the bears do, which was not a pretty sight—and, besides, more rain was coming. So after hanging around for a while, I decided to head back home and wait for the album and movie.

So yes, I made it to Woodstock, more than once, and am apparently memorialized there, but I never shared the experiences of Frank and Billy and Bob and other friends who hitched up Friday and ended up stuck, albeit gloriously, for all three days. They truly experienced what one could arguably call the greatest musical happening of all time, even if they spent practically the entire time sopping wet, freezing in the cold night air, hungry, thirsty, and covered in mud.

Coda: A decade-and-a-half later, as a reporter for Newsweek, I met Steve Ross, the legendary chairman of Warner Bros., who built it into the international music/movie/video/television network colossus it is today. He told me that when he bought Warner Bros. in 1969, he only wanted the record label and planned on dumping the movie and television divisions. Instead, an old friend, agent Ted Ashley, convinced him to give the movie division one last shot.

And the first picture released after Ross took over . . .

Woodstock. And it became such a hit it not only saved the division, it ignited Warner's climb to its top slot in the world media business today.

If you add that in, you might say that my Woodstock experience was memorable on a lot of levels—viscerally and existentially—and if, in fact, I am in the movie . . . where are my damn residuals?

The late Peter McAlevey was a motion picture producer who released twenty-four movies in his career, including Screamers, Shadow Hours, Klash, Flatliners, Double Impact, and Stone Cold. As a former Vice President of Production at both Walt Disney Pictures and Michael Douglas' production company, he executive produced Radio Flyer and Hard Promises. McAlevey also spent many years as an internationally known journalist for Newsweek, The New York Times, Los Angeles Times, Businessweek, and Forbes.

With the Film Crew

By Catherine Hiller

As each day passed, my anxiety grew. For weeks, my boyfriend, Stan, and I had known about the music festival with its incredible line-up of talent—The Jefferson Airplane! The Who! Jimi Hendrix! Janis Joplin! The Band! I wanted to snap up tickets, even though they would have cost $36 for the two of us. But Stan had heard rumblings that the Woodstock producers might film the festival and hoped they would need him to shoot, which meant we'd go for free.

In 1969, I dressed the part of a hippie, wearing blue-tinted John Lennon glasses, bell-bottom jeans, with tight T-shirts or gauzy Indian tops. In reality, I was a "weekend hippie," or maybe more accurately, a "fashion hippie." True, I demonstrated against the Vietnam War and counseled draft resisters; true, I supported civil rights and tutored in a black neighborhood; and true, I certainly loved smoking pot. But I admired rational thought, planned to earn a doctorate, worked hard for my grades, and ate meat. What I revered about the counterculture was its music, songs that inspired me to protest and to dance, music that was relevant and inventive and radically different from the lovesick laments of the past.

Just days before the festival, Warner Brothers invested $25,000 for production and hired Michael Wadleigh, known in downtown New York as a brilliant cinematographer, to direct a documentary of the festival. The call went out for people with 16 mm cameras to help shoot, and Stan was in. With any luck, we thought at the time, this film could be as good as Monterey Pop, and rumor had it that Bob Dylan himself might appear.

When we arrived on Thursday, Stan shot footage of kids dancing and smoking pot; at night, we returned to the motel, where we slept in dry rooms on clean sheets. Every morning, I set up the ironing board and ironed my hair. In those days it was very important to have long, perfectly straight hair, although the iron sometimes left burn marks on my arms.

Stan was assigned to a platform to one side of the main stage, high up on a tower. Three main cameras close to the stage covered each performer, bolstered by several cameras shooting from other angles. We didn't have the traditional slate or clapper-board, so Stan scribbled the name of the group on a sheet of paper and shot me holding it up to mark the beginning of their performance. I distinctly remember displaying his scrawled sign for Santana.

The music was astonishing and sounded great: whether you were next to the stage or standing a quarter mile away you could hear the lead guitars dueling against the basses. When I wasn't on the platform helping Stan, or simply watching the concert—agog—I sat beneath the stage with the other cameramen's girlfriends and assistants, changing magazines. Each reel of 16 mm film lasted eleven minutes, and we had to change each magazine by transferring exposed film into a can and loading new film into the camera.

When the rain returned, the mud mingled with the cow-pasture manure, creating a horrendous smell, but everyone remained cheerful, light-hearted. Chip Monk, the mellifluous MC, told us we'd closed down the New York Thruway. He told us not to take the brown acid—not because it was illegal, but because it was a bummer. When he announced Joan Baez and she began to sing, I felt as if Lady Madonna herself serenaded us, her voice like clear water over stones. When Crosby, Stills, Nash & Young (whose first album had just come out and whose every song I knew by heart) came to the stage, they confessed that it was their second public performance and that they were "scared shitless." Shitless! I loved their brute honesty and profanity. I loved that the performers and stagehands and audience all wore the same clothes. I loved the convergence: young people with the same politics, outrage and values all gathered together, half a million strong, supporting each other.

Stan went on to become one of the editors of Woodstock, as well as my husband. An earlier version of Santana's performance began with me holding up that piece of paper, but when the director asked Stan to re-cut the sequence, this opening did not jibe with Stan's vision, so he removed it. At the time, I was very proud of Stan—his aesthetic had trumped the personal; but now, all these years (and one divorce) later, I'm no longer happy that he left me on the cutting room floor. Woodstock, the film, chronicled my generation's pivotal event, and I wish I had my second onscreen: young, grinning, straight hair flying in the wind.

Catherine Hiller is a novelist, filmmaker, and book editor (www.executiveeditor.com). Her proudest achievement is being the mother of three idealistic young men. They and she are Burning Man enthusiasts.

Susan Reynolds

August is My Summer of '69
By John Bianco with Jon Jaboolian

In the summer of 1969, I had just finished my first year of college and, like many other college students, was sent home early. All over the country, students had increasingly protested the Vietnam War by taking over their schools, or sections of their schools, for a few hours—or a few days. At Oneonta, in upstate New York, I had been part of the human barricades that blocked the classroom buildings. The final resistance had taken place at the administration building, where we convinced them to shut down the school in time for student dissenters to travel down to Washington, D.C to participate in an anti-war march.

I had gone home feeling suffused with a sense of unity, and the only reason I didn't go to D.C for the march was that my father had secured me a job in construction that summer, and I couldn't let him down.

As the summer progressed, I read about an "Aquarian Exposition— Celebrating 3 Days of Peace & Music" and decided it was exactly what I needed. My friends Jon Jaboolian, Billy Ortega, and I all bought tickets and convinced Billy's father to let us drive his family's new 1969 Chevelle station wagon to the festival.

Friday afternoon, August 15, we struck out for what we thought would be three lazy days of music in the country. Not long after, we began hearing news reports on the car radio that the New York State Thruway was backed up, so we swung onto Route 9 to Newburg, and then cut west from there. We knew we were getting close when abandoned cars lined the road and throngs of hippies (and a lot of pretty straight looking teens), with knapsacks and sleeping bags slung over their shoulders, filed steadily in one direction. We inched slowly forward for hours, until we realized we were at the intersection of Hurd Road and West Shore Drive, smack in the middle of the festival site. When Jon asked someone where the stage was, the guy shook his head and answered, "Hey man, right there!" It was the length of a football field away.

According to Jon (who remembers everything) The Incredible String Band had just taken the stage, but almost immediately thereafter the skies opened up, and the band ran for cover . . . and so did we. We stayed in our car that night but didn't get much sleep much because folks were roaming up and down Hurd Road in close proximity to our car throughout the night.

Around daybreak, the road cleared a bit, revealing an empty field to our right that had a stone wall around it and an opening to allow vehicles to pass, so we fired up the Chevelle and drove through it—right up to Max Yasgur's home. We didn't know that it was his house, of course, but felt lucky to have found a quiet, private spot to park our car.

We had just settled in for a little shuteye when wind whipped up around us so violently, it rocked the car back and forth. We opened up the windows of the wagon and discovered a helicopter hovering directly above us, and a passenger gesturing wildly for us to move the hell out of the way. Because of the clogged roads, the organizers had to shuttle the bands on and off the site via helicopter, and it seems that we had inadvertently parked on the helicopter pad.

After moving the car, and cooking breakfast on a small Coleman-type stove, Billy and I went to check things out, and when we came back, Jon said two freaks had shown up with about twenty pounds of chopped meat from their father's butcher store and needed to cook the stuff before it spoiled. Jon helped them cook burgers, and they fed a whole bunch of folks.

We stayed until Sunday afternoon, and although it all blurred over the passage of time, what I remember most is being shoulder-to-shoulder with hundreds of thousands of tired, hungry, wet, mud-covered, and thirsty people, and not seeing one act of violence. Instead, I saw food being passed around freely—sandwiches being passed from person to person, with each person taking a small bite before passing it on to the stranger beside him. Everyone was sharing everything. Even the concession stands—like the ticket-takers—gave up any idea of charging for anything and began giving away whatever food they had.

I left Woodstock with a sense of purpose and belonging that has remained alive in me to this day. Between the anti-war protests and being one of hundreds of thousands gathered on Max Yasgur's farm, I felt part of something big, something I had no idea at the time would have such far-reaching consequences.

Recently, when my twelve-year-old son, John, discovered—on his own—how great the music of my generation was compared to what he hears today, he asked me endless questions about the bands, the music, the times, and, of course, Woodstock. My coolness factor ratcheted up considerably when he learned that I was actually one of "those hippies." He and I watched the Woodstock film together, and then he downloaded songs to his I-pod. Of course, like us, he really responded to the "Fish Cheer."

Obviously, Woodstock was a trip, and lest I forget one single minute of it, Jon calls me—and Billy—on the anniversary to marvel a bit at how lucky we were to be there. But Jon knew that long ago—he had taken down the address of the Yasgur house, and when he got home, sent the Yasgurs a card thanking them for their hospitality.

John Bianco is an award-winning TV and film director with years of experience directing and producing numerous high profile network programs and news specials. Documentary credits include: Adventures in Space with Leonard Nimoy, Disaster Chronicles, Portraits of American Presidents, America: A Look Back, and The Story of Washington, D.C. Jon Jaboolian is a live sound engineer and sound designer living in south Florida.

The Top of the Psychedelic Food Chain

By Brian King

I spent the summer of 1968 living in Oregon, hanging out with the Grateful Dead and Ken Kesey's Merry Pranksters. My girlfriend, Katie Scott, had grown up in California, with parents who were friends with Joan Baez, Kesey, and The Grateful Dead. That summer, I hitched from Long Island to California to meet up with Katie, who had flown west to spend time with her grandmother in Coronado.

George Walker, one of the Merry Pranksters, drove to Coronado in a white Cadillac he had just inherited. George and a friend planned to travel around the world in a 60-foot sailboat, and they invited Katie and I to go along—at least for a portion of the journey. I don't remember why, but George, Katie, and I bailed at the first Mexican port of call, retrieved the Caddy, and drove up Route 1 to San Francisco, where we hung out with The Dead.

The Dead practiced in an old church where the altars and pews had been removed, leaving a wide expanse with a balcony above it. Groupies were always hanging around, mostly girls with long flowing blonde hair—braless girls wearing tie-dye skirts so long they drug on the floor. These lovely girls circulated regularly, carrying trays loaded with drug offerings. It was the sixties, man. Some sampled the drugs, and some didn't. Eventually, Jerry Garcia and his band of brothers would pick up their instruments and treat us to their forever-unfolding musical journey. By mid-afternoon the church was rocking, and kept on rocking well into the night.

George wanted to head up to Oregon, so Katie and I went along and stayed for two months. In truth, my memories of those days are fuzzy. I remember Kesey as an oddball character, strolling around, and even riding his tractor wearing only red, polka dot boxers, and a red bandana tied around his head. I also remember the day we all unknowingly swallowed something stronger than usual and tripped for eighteen hours. And days we swam naked in a waterfall. And then the day I caught George and Katie in bed—together. The next day I hitched a ride down to San Francisco, and from there home.

Katie and I broke up officially later that year; thus, the summer of 1969 found me fresh out of high school and feeling oddly independent and trapped. As a conscientious objector searching for truth in the world, I had spent months actively seeking sponsors who would write glowing character references that I could use to stave off the draft board and stay the hell out of Vietnam.

My fate was up in the air when I went to Woodstock with Bill Evans, Steve Ramerez, and Peter Beh, members of a Long Island rock band. We took the train as far as we could, and then hitched. Once there, we tramped a mile into the woods where we thought we could carve out a private campsite. We cut branches to place under our tent to cushion our sleeping bags, and constructed wood huts to protect our stuff in case of rain. Peter couldn't handle the steadily growing crowd and split. That left Bill, Steve, and me to have all the fun.

Later Friday morning I went in search of the Kesey bus, Further, which I heard was making the trip. Within a short time, I located the bus, glowing in the sunlight. With its flowing psychedelic images covering every surface of the bus, that sucker must have looked like an acid comet coming down the highway. Typical of their lunacy, the Pranksters had tied welding tanks on the back of the bus and filled them with nitrous oxide, and during the three or four hours I hung around, someone randomly tossed out handfuls of acid every few hours. Inside the bus, mattresses lined the floors and every inch of wall space contained scrawled sayings or drawings that obviously reflected whatever "trip" the "artist" was on at the time. Groupies hung around for hours, listening to the Prankster tales.

Saturday morning, Bill, Steve, and I made it our goal to edge down as close as we could to the front of the main stage. Eventually, we inched our way within 200 feet of the stage, where we hunkered down for the duration, as did everyone else.

The music was unbelievable, of course, but I found the massive audience far more fascinating. I stared at them everywhere I went—and I went everywhere. I must have walked fifty miles in those four days, and would have walked a ton more, if the rain, a bout of dysentery (from failing to boil the lake water long enough before cooking our rations), and their combined effects hadn't spoiled my natural (and occasionally unnatural) high.

We left Sunday, knowing full well that we had experienced something amazing, something that was never to happen again on that scale. But the best news came when I got home. I had been awarded a 4F based on my strong moral objections to war. A 4F meant that Uncle Sam would draft my grandmother before they drafted me. I was thrilled that I didn't have to leave the country I loved, that I didn't have to betray my own convictions, and that I didn't have to fight in Vietnam. Far out.

Brian King is a slightly reformed hippie who has never forgotten his roots. After traveling the world, he settled down with a mid-western wife and had two daughters. Today, Brian lives a remarkably normal life in Charleston, South Carolina.

Opposite Poles

By Janine Fleury

As a recent immigrant from communist Poland, I was anxious to experience the America I had heard about in my childhood village of Novogrod. The upcoming Woodstock music festival seemed the perfect place to begin my journey. With my boyfriend, Peter, we made the trek from Wilmington, Delaware, to the Mecca of the American counterculture movement. I looked the part of a hippie, clad in plaid bell-bottoms with more hues than Joseph's Technicolor coat, a skin-tight yellow halter-top, and a flowered bandana.

I knew something about living off the land, specifically the woods around my village in Poland's lake region. If I hadn't learned early on to forage for mushrooms, cattails, stinging nettle, and the many other edible plants and berries necessary to supplement our diets, I likely would not have survived to adulthood. I already understood that one eats to live, not the other way around.

Like many of the young people attending Woodstock, Peter and I had made no plans for meals or hotel accommodations. We had no money anyway. Since all the campsites were full, we pitched our tent in the woods. The next morning, we walked for miles along the narrow roads, following endless lines of parked cars and Volkswagen buses, some gaudily decorated with giant sunflowers and peace signs. Finally, we reached Max Yasgur's farm to join in the celebration.

Perched atop Peter's shoulders, I saw tens of thousands of heads, looking very much like the cobblestones in my village streets. What I saw next blew my mind far more than any LSD trip Timothy Leary ever described: Hundreds of thousands began chanting anti-war slogans, some even waved placards protesting the war. Fear raced through my veins. In my country, everyone—demonstrators and innocent bystanders alike—would have been immediately arrested, or worse. For a while, I could scarcely breathe, but none of these protesters appeared concerned . . . not a trace of fear showed on anyone's faces. Slowly, I relaxed enough to hear the music again. What a country America was shaping up to be.

Camping the night before had led to another new American experience: poison ivy. I had never heard of poison ivy in Novogrod, but it found me in upstate New York, with a vengeance. It was everywhere, in my ears, on my eyelids, even on my . . . well, you get the picture. Somehow, it didn't matter.

My newly found sense of freedom, compounded by the music, produced an indescribable high. Since childhood I had trained as a dancer, and suddenly I longed to dance. Since there was barely room to stand, with me still on his shoulders, Peter elbowed his way through the crowd to the base of a nearby hill. After climbing to the top, we found grass and empty space. I danced, barefoot, as Richie Havens's guitar and gravelly voice filled the air with Motherless Child. Later, when we moved in closer once again, music blaring from enormous speakers mingled with drifting fogs of marijuana smoke and the malty aroma of beer produced my first—and last—taste of Reefer Madness.

A few years later, Peter and I parted ways and married other people. Nearly four decades have passed since those idyllic days at Woodstock, yet I remember the crowds of hippies and hippie-wannabes, and our idealism and naïve desire to live in a world ruled by peace, love, limitless freedom, and respect for one's environment. For many of my contemporaries, I suspect Woodstock was the defining experience of their lives, a reconnection with some Eden-like natural world most had experienced only in their dreams.

It was also so for me, yet I always had mixed feelings about the whole experience. Growing up, malnutrition and tuberculosis were my constant companions so I knew from experience that living off the land was not always as romantic as it seemed. I knew that a steady diet of sour grass soup, boiled nettle, and sleeping under the stars would have cured most erstwhile flower children—myself included—of our longing for a return to nature.

In the months following Woodstock, Max Yasgur's dairy farm lay in ruins, and his neighbors sued him for damage to neighboring properties. Three years later, he died of a heart attack. Was that the price he paid? I don't know, but I mourned the destruction of his property—his Eden.

Janine Fleury is a retired foreign language teacher, writer, and health food advocate. Janine is also an accomplished runner and veteran of sixteen marathons, often finishing first in her age group—now sixty. Her article, "A Small World," covering the Warsaw Marathon, in which she also competed, was published in Running Times Magazine.

The Little Car that Could

By Michael Sciulla

Little did Ralph Nader know when he penned his 1965 expose of the American automobile industry, "Unsafe at Any Speed," that the funky Corvair he panned would end up a hero at Woodstock four years later.

On a beautiful summer's day, Thursday, August 14 to be exact, about ten of my buddies and I hit the road in three cars from East Meadow, Long Island to crash a concert in upstate NewYork. Everyone who was anyone was going, and we were all hot to have one final fling before our freshman year in college, before life began in earnest.

Four of us piled into my 1962 fire-engine red Corvair and hopped on the Long Island Distressway where we eventually crossed the bridges that bound our suburban homeland to the wider world and put us on the New York Thruway and Route 17 that would eventually take us to upstate New York and Max Yasgur's farm.

Mind you, while most of us had flown to other parts of the country with our parents on holiday, few of us had much experience traveling any appreciable distance from home in our own cars. The longest distance we'd ever traveled was probably fifty miles out to the Hamptons to party and hang out with the crowd following the Hassels, a band with a keyboardist named Billy Joel.

None of us had any experience traversing Route 17, the east-west highway that meandered uphill through the lower Catskills.

As our caravan climbed the mountains, about two hours from home, we heard radio reports of tens of thousands of hippies converging on the music festival, and warnings from the announcers that the authorities might turn everyone away and close the festival.

Around that same time, we were rapidly losing forward momentum as we climbed one of the steeper mountains along Route 17. While we had been cruising along at a comfortable 60 mph, our speed went steadily downhill, from 55 mph to 50 mph to 45 mph, when panic set in. What was wrong with the car? Were we going to break down less than an hour from our destination?

Sweat began to pour as we approached the mountain's peak. Using gallows humor, one of my friends observed that if we made it to the mountaintop we could put the car in neutral and coast all the way to the gates of Woodstock. We never had to test that possibility because as soon as our Corvair eased over the mountaintop, we picked up speed, and life returned to normal. Only then did we realize that nothing was wrong and that the seriously underpowered Corvair just didn't have enough power to haul four kids up any mountain at 60 mph.

Arriving at the festival grounds, we parked the car in one of Max Yasgur's fields, set up our tents and joined upwards of a half million hippies. What transpired over the next four days has pretty much been lost to the fog of time. All that remains are imprecise memories of sitting on that sloping field for the better part of eighty hours listening to unbelievable music and watching legendary artists in the heat, rain, and mud of mid-August.

Having said that, some memories do remain and are more vivid than others: Richie Havens' electrifying performance of "Freedom" reflected the tenor of the times; Joe Cocker was absolutely manic; Country Joe and the Fish got the crowd rockin with "Rock and Soul Music"; Crosby, Stills, Nash and Young's "Suite: Judy Blue Eyes" brought the crowd to its feet, and Jimi Hendrix playing "The Star-Spangled Banner" brought the house down.

When the concert ended, the prospect of joining a half million people on Route 17 had little appeal. Instead, we decided to stay an extra few days and enjoy what was left of the experience. This included watching farm tractors tow hundreds of cars out of the muddy fields.

When we decided to leave, we simply fired up the little red Corvair, and—thanks to GM's decision to put the car's engine in the rear where its weight gave us all the traction we needed—drove right out. The vehicle's earlier shortcomings were forgiven.

I ended up spending more money to buy the Woodstock album and see the movie than I did during the week I hung out at Max Yasgur's farm. It just goes to show that some of the best things in life are free.

Michael Sciulla was lounging on the deck of a multi-million yacht at the Ft. Lauderdale Boat Show when told his tale would appear in this anthology. For nearly three years, Sciulla has been a lobbyist for Boat Owners Association of The United States and editor and publisher of Boat U.S. Magazine. As a lobbyist, he has testified before Congress more than thirty times. As a magazine editor, however, he feels compelled to note that the aforementioned yacht was not his.

When I was Fifteen

By Linda W. Hamilton

I hitchhiked from Alexandria, Virginia, to Woodstock with my seventeen-year-old brother, Tony. I had heard a rumor that Dylan was going to be there, and with that news, I decided I was going to be there too. So I scrounged up a waitress job in a filthy snack bar at National Airport (working the 3 P.M. to 11 P.M. shift for $1.35 an hour) to pay our way to Woodstock.

I wasn't exactly naïve. At age fourteen, I had been arrested on Pennsylvania Avenue for participating in an anti-war protest during Nixon's inauguration. My picture—literally being carried away by two policemen—graced the front page of one of the Washington Post's sections the next morning. I still recall the chant of the day: "LSD, Let's Screw Dick!" Prior to this, I had organized a demonstration at the Canadian embassy to protest the slaughtering of fur seals. I had stuffed my fair share of envelopes for presidential contender Eugene McCarthy. I had also been pelted with my fair share of grapes and lettuce while demonstrating in support of migrant farm workers at the Safeway adjacent to my school. Jocks did the pelting. After the riots in 1968, I spent many hours in the D.C ghetto tie-dying T-shirts for the neighborhood children.

Tony and I arrived in Bethel days before the concert was set to begin. We assumed we would be able to hitch to town and buy food, and, picturing warm, sunny days spent communing with nature and nights spent sleeping under the stars, we had come seriously under-prepared. We each had a blanket, and the clothing we wore on our backs, in my case: jeans, a T-shirt, boots, and a green, knee-length, long-sleeved army jacket purchased at Sunny Surplus in Georgetown. I also had a brown paper grocery sack filled with sanitary napkins. I had only been having periods for a few months, and was still a novice at womanhood.

The days of the concert are blurred together in my memory. But I can tell you this: it rained, it rained, it rained. There was no shelter, so Tony and I accepted being wet, wetter, and even wetter. Somehow we managed to rest curled up on our blankets. The downpours saturated my paper bag of napkins, which created major worry. Fortunately, a first aid booth opened, and when news of it spread, I scrambled over there for dry supplies. I shyly—and I thought slyly—requested "feminine products." The fellow gave me tampons, something I had never used, did not know how to use. I returned to the booth to exchange the tampons for napkins and hid in the shadows several hours until the male volunteer was relieved by a female, and then made the exchange feeling true relief.

People started arriving en masse. All kinds of people from everywhere descended on the farm. The bright colored clothing worn on the close-knit human bodies smeared the landscape like a crazy quilt. With the population increase, Tony and I could no longer hitch into town to buy food. No one was going anywhere, and we began to get hungry. But all those who had anything to eat shared what they had with those who had nothing. A pretty flower child with long, flowing hair, fed me strawberry jam with a spoon. Sweet! Then of course there was the Hog Farm commune, which set up a kitchen and served some necessarily creative, and very welcome cuisine.

Thankfully, when it really started to rain hard, Tony and I were hanging out with people who had a large tent with mattresses in it. One of the guys said I could sleep with him. After nights spent curled on my blanket, I jumped at the chance for some dry comfort, though I wondered what was in store. I retired wearing all my clothes, including boots and army jacket, and slept peacefully, lulled by the sound of steady drops hitting the canvas.

The music played at Woodstock over the three days proved phenomenal. Tony and I saw every performer. One memorable moment was spelling with Country Joe and the Fish. "Give me an F!" Can you imagine the thrill of hearing a half million people—pissed off about Vietnam—yelling out replies?

We departed Woodstock Monday morning shortly after Hendrix played The Star Spangled Banner. By this time, the only thing I had on was the army jacket; everything else had rotted away in the rain. Fortunately my period had ended. The first car that stopped could only accommodate one, so Tony urged me to take the ride. I rode home with three or four guys, one of whom was named Charlie. We stopped for a meal of chipped beef on toast in Lancaster, Pennsylvania, at one of the guy's sister's, Charlie's, I think, and then headed south to Alexandria. The week at Woodstock had come to an end though it signified a beginning. I had no idea that history had been made until after I was back home and heard the news. The experience definitely helped define who I am today. Woodstock taught me to share myself and to abstain from judging others–to meet folks where they are instead of where I'd like them to be, or imagine them to be—pretty good lessons for a fifteen-year-old.

Linda Hamilton has a master's degree in social work and works as a medical social worker in home health services. She lives in a rural area in Virginia close to the Chesapeake Bay. A high school writer friend contacted her and urged her to submit a piece for the Woodstock Revisited writing opportunity.

The Yin Yang of the Summer of '69
By Phil Vinall

Like Kerouac, my generation was coming and going at the speed of sound. The sound of Dylan, The Stones, and The Beatles was always with us, with us in those small California towns of La Jolla, Seal, and Redondo Beach, in the back-bay rentals of North Wildwood, New Jersey, and in our cars and vans speeding from one state to the next. And when we stopped moving from here to there and back again, it poured out of the hip clubs—Elfreth's Alley, the Gilded Gage, and the Electric Factory in my Philadelphia—and the lofts and houses in whatever cities we called home.

Inhaling anything a match could ignite, we floated on the edge of a moment in time. In the vein of those comedic Fabulous Furry Freak Brothers much of life consisted of searching for and enjoying recreational, mind-blowing drugs:

"Dope will get you through times of no money better than money will get you through times of no dope."

—Freewheelin' Franklin

When we weren't stoned, and sometimes when we were, we protested the draft, the war, or the bad food at the university, even though we weren't officially students.

We had nothing, and we needed nothing. We lived without thinking about the future, without paying bills, without buying a new car, and without getting that next promotion. In fact, few of us had real jobs. Life is cheap, life is easy, we believed.

But by the summer of 1969 we were growing tired and feeling old; the protests, the riots, and the assassination of our heroes kept coming and coming.

When we weren't talking about the impending revolution we were talking about moving to the country, to another country, sometimes even to another world, a la Jefferson Airplane in HiJack the Starship, who advocated traveling past the sun to another universe. I was feeling very alone. She had left with the others a while ago.

July 21, 1969. Neil Armstrong walked on the moon, and we sat, eyes glued to our television. One of my friends—convinced the moon landing would spark the interstellar community to contact us at any minute and reveal all the extraterrestrial secrets we needed to become star travelers—waited on the roof of our house, ready and watching.

August 1-3, 1969. 100,000 of us gathered at The Atlantic City Pop Festival, to hear the The Byrds, Canned Heat, Joe Cocker, Iron Butterfly, and Janis Joplin. As good as it was, word around the track was if you think this is good, wait until Woodstock. Despite spotty advertisement, word of the impending mega-festival traveled north, south, east, and west on the psychedelic underground grapevine. The Hog Farm, North Star, and other famous communes began loading their psychedelic buses for the long journey east.

Along with the others, She boarded a bus in Taos.

August 8, 1969. Tex and a few of Charlie's girls, Sadie Mae, Patricia, and Linda, spent the night carving up the Tate family. Charles Manson blamed the Beatles' White Album for telling him to start "Helter Skelter."

I packed a small duffel, wondering (worrying) what ever happened to peace and love.

August 15, 1969. Woodstock began, and hit the news hard. The more we saw scenes of the clogged traffic, heard police warnings not to come, or saw and heard the locals saying that they were running out of food and other supplies, the more we had to be there.

Interstate 87 was jammed in the Central Valley area. Police urged us to turn around and go home, so we linked up with strangers, fellow journeymen, who had local maps. After scary backroad driving and one brief foray through a cow pasture, we got within five miles of the site, at which point we abandoned our cars and started walking.

After hours of uncertainty, we realized we were going to make it to the greatest music festival ever, and our mood bordered on jovial. Fellow walkers passed joints back along the line, and closer in, we could hear music far off in the distance.

Reaching the rim of a large valley, I looked out at the mass of people. It took my breath away. At the bottom, a huge stage, topped with a flapping, bright white, tent-like structure, beckoned. Thousands of lights flickered; people smiled, kissed, lay wrapped in each other's arms, or gyrated to the music. An underground/aboveground earth rhythm felt tangible, almost visible to many, and very visible, very tangible to those tripping as the twilight closed around us.

Tucked into the woods, logs and trees with bent and braided limbs formed natural individual enclosures for the inhabitants of Dealer's Alley, who shouted out the names of their products—Window Pane, rare Owsley acid, Karoline's Kief, Chihuahuan mescal buttons, shrooms, and others I've long forgotten.

And then . . .

She stood in small group, a joint going clockwise, and a bottle of Boone's Farm going counterclockwise.

"Did you come for me?" She asked.

"Yes," I replied.

Much has changed since then. Soon, using drugs became more about tuning out than tuning in. The revolution never happened, and we didn't end up on a starship, propelling ourselves into space. Rock and roll did fade away, but the music never died.

And neither did we.

Phil Vinall is a medical writer who lives in West Chester, Pennsylvania, with his wife of forty years. He held her hand as they buried her mother, as She gave birth, as they removed the cancer from her breast. He holds her hand still.

Peace, Man

By R.G. Nourse

I know she saw me; she looked right at me, as she pulled out right in front of me in her little black sedan. I thought about not braking, just plowing into her car. Instead, I braked, grateful there was no one behind me to slam into the rear of my car, and shouted "Ass-ho" before clamping my mouth shut. I'm a kinder, gentler person these days, thanks in part to the peace-love-freedom-and-happiness groove I've been working under since the mid-1960s.

In the 1960s, I was a skinny little blonde who walked around with her head in the clouds, naïve but curious about everything. It was the '60s, man, and I had it down. Okay, maybe I wasn't as hip as I thought.

By mid-August 1969, I was a bit more tuned in. I'd attended at least half a dozen anti-war rallies on the Mall in Washington, D.C. I'd dropped out of college after my first year. I was trying to "find myself," just like a few million other people around the world. I was living at my dad's house and hanging out with a group who lived together in a house in Arlington, Virginia, just across the D.C. line. We'd meet each night after work for dinner, beer, wine, and joints. On the weekends, sometimes, Chaz would come through town with a suitcase full of Owlsley acid that he'd brought from California.

Suki's boyfriend, Bruce, told us one night about the Woodstock Music & Art Festival that was coming up. So many groups were expected to appear: The Who, Jefferson Airplane, the Grateful Dead, Santana, Sly and the Family Stone, and more and more and more. He'd heard that Bob Dylan "would probably" show up and maybe even John Lennon.

Well, who could say no to that lineup? Since going to the National Teen Show at the D.C. Armory in 1966, I'd been a sucker for live music. Even before that, my older brother played in R & B bands locally and I'd dated a drummer in a garage band (Nils Lofgren played with them occasionally. Back then, he was a shy little kid who just wanted to play rock 'n roll so they let him).

We left D.C. the day before it began. Suki, Bruce, and I rode while John; my boyfriend did the driving. John and Bruce were brothers who had grown up in New York State and said they knew where Woodstock was taking place. The festival had been moved to Bethel, New York, a couple of weeks before.

We actually did meet up with our friends, somehow finding them mixed in with the hundreds of people shuffling along the road. I turned nineteen that day, and we set up a cargo parachute to use as a tent. The rain poured down, destroying our home-away-from-home. We packed up our food and sleeping bags and headed out, following the sound of the roadies running sound checks. Through the woods and up a hill we walked. We reached the top and peered over into a natural amphitheatre.

What an amazing sight. Thousands and thousands of people just like us: Long hair, blue jeans, and everyone smiling. A stage with towers of amplifiers reaching to the sky lay at the bottom of the bowl. Un-fucking-believable. I'm sure someone coined that phrase at Woodstock.

Everywhere I looked, I saw people sharing what food and drink they'd brought. When the music stopped for the night, I heard low voices, laughter, and people making love under their blankets. Far away from any city lights, the Milky Way was a definite streak across the night sky. An occasional shooting star added to the magic.

By Saturday afternoon, everyone had settled in. If you've seen the movie, remember that it was filmed around the perimeter, along the edges. And edges don't tell the story about the middle. We sat in the middle of it all, a group of seven amid half a million. I'd look out over that mass of happy people and say, "Wow!" Then, five other people nearby would do the same and echo, "Wow!"

No one stepped on your stuff, unless they were a little too high. People would walk by the edge of your blanket and say, "Excuse me." And smile. Sure everyone was mellow, but the vibe emanated love.

Sometime during Sunday afternoon, we heard a guy begin yelling behind us. Another man answered in anger. Within minutes, a circle of smiling, happy people had formed around them. Someone began to chant, "No more war, man! No more war." It quickly grew into a larger group, encircling the two men in peace and love. "No more war, man! No more war." They hugged each other and laughed, then a girl offered a beer, and it was back to "Peace, man."

To this day, I can picture the crowd, hear the music, and feel that incredible vibration of peace, love, freedom, and happiness. When some woman drives crazily, like today, I begin to freak—I almost go there— and then I make that V with my fingers. Instead of "the bird," I shoot her the peace sign. Peace, man.

R.G. Nourse is a political activist, now living in the Southeast corner of Washington State. From her start in Washington, D.C., through Maryland, Virginia, Texas, and Idaho, she's been an observer of America and its inhabitants' way of life. Now less-abled by multiple sclerosis, her website is http://MSNourse.com.

One Way or Another

By S.K. List

I still have my tickets—clean and unused. They should probably be in a frame, but they're buried somewhere in my house, with lots of other good stuff. We bought them by mail after we saw the full-page ads in the New York papers, and we were looking forward to a great party.

I was married, just twenty-two, and living in Gettysburg, Pennsylvania, in a ground-floor apartment right across the street from Gettysburg College, from which my husband and I had both recently graduated. We had a dark green, 1949 Chevy truck that we called "The Groundhog." I walked to work at a feed store up the street, and he drove to his job with the local roofers. The Friday of the festival, we got out of work early and ran around gathering what we thought we needed. God only knows what that was. I'm sure we thought we were well prepared, but was anyone? Blankets? Maybe. I don't think we even owned sleeping bags. Food? Maybe. Change of clothes? Toothbrushes? I guess, and, oh, yeah, our tickets. Then we set off.

We got as far as Harrisburg, about thirty miles away, and The Groundhog expired by the side of the road.

Somehow we called a friend who came and pulled the truck to a repair shop in Gettysburg, where we tried to impress the owner with a sense of urgency. I can picture The Groundhog with one end propped up on a floor jack in the big old-fashioned garage. The dying sunlight is shining through a wall of factory-style windows, and the guy is saying, "It's the transmission." Somehow, he was telling us that, urgency or not, our trip was just not gonna happen.

For the rest of the weekend, we listened, like lost explorers on the other end of a crackling short wave, to bulletins about the festival streaming in over the radio. Even with the mechanic's dire prognosis, I think that, for most of the next day—even into Sunday—we somehow thought we would get there. But increasingly, the radio spread the message, like that sign in The Wizard of Oz: "If I were you, I'd turn back now." Even if we didn't hear it directly from Arlo, we got the word: "The New York State Thruway is closed, man."

We sat in the back yard of our apartment building, playing all our favorite albums on speakers aimed out the kitchen window, mourning as we grasped that we were missing the event that, even more than the anti-war marches we'd been to in D.C. and New York, was turning out to be the landmark of a generation.

Our building housed a mix of students and families, but in summer most of the students were gone and, at our end of town, away from the central battlefield and Gettysburg's tourists, the pace was lazy and peaceful. Our kitchen door and the neighbors' opened right onto a few wooden steps down into the back yard, so we had claimed that space, hanging up a string of plastic used-car-lot pennants for festivity, giving dinner parties, and hanging out there all the time.

In the apartment alongside ours were two football players, people we never would have expected to become our friends, but we found out they were two of the sweetest guys in the world. One of the guys was the football team captain and, with all that grace and strength and agility, he was—astoundingly—getting into dance. Another evening that summer, he had taken us to the sun-dappled shade of the Old Quad across the street and, spinning, leaping like a faun amongst the trees and sun-shafts there, he had improvised a glorious freeform ballet just for us. All kinds of things were changing that summer.

I don't really regret missing Woodstock. In time, I got muddy and danced at some other very big festivals and concerts, including the humungous 1973 Summer Jam in Watkins Glen. It surpassed Woodstock in head-count and matched it for bad weather, bad planning, and good vibes. Even with all the hassles, I had a terrific time.

I see Woodstock as the beginning of the counterculture's inclination to go back to the land, and that's something I've learned to value permanently here in my home in beautiful upstate New York, not far from Watkins Glen or Woodstock. That grew directly out of summer 1969. For me, against all the turmoil in the world outside, that summer was an idyll in a beautiful place, in the Pennsylvania countryside. I t taught me a way of daily life—cooking meals, eating outside, loving music, hanging out with friends—that is at the core of the social values I still embrace. I think that even if I'd made it to Woodstock, I couldn't hold any closer the goals and ideals that informed the cultural movement it symbolizes. The goodness that marked Woodstock came, in part, from young people learning in a group how to value simple things and work together for the benefit of all.

By the time we visited Woodstock, New York, it was just a hippie town full of crystals for tourists, vegetarian restaurants, and imaginary Dylan sightings. But as the Dead say, "One way or another . . . " As much of a kick as I would have gotten out of actually being at Yasgur's farm, I'm thankful to be able to say I didn't have to be there to learn its lessons.

S.K. List is a writer, editor, and former journalist living in Trumansburg, New York. She has been a goat farmer, blacksmith, painter, publisher, and hippie-communard. Her work has appeared in The New York Times, American Demographics, Rock & Roll Confidential, and alternative weeklies across the country.

Susan Reynolds

Music, Dope, and Good Times
By Pam Crowe-Weisberg

As it proved for many in my generation—and the world—the summer of 1969 was a time of major change. I was about to graduate from college in January, a transfer from the University of Colorado to NYU at the end of my sophomore year. I had grown up in a quintessential middle class neighborhood in Westchester County. I had been co-captain of the high school cheerleading team, and had dated the captain of the football team since my freshman year, and I had remained close with my high school friends. From the start, we had been torn about Vietnam—some had been radically opposed; others had been in strong favor. By1969, all of us were against the war. Several of my friends had been drafted; a few had died.

None of us were hippies in the true sense, but we loved music, dope, and good times. A bunch of us decided to make the trek to Bethel. We arrived early and found a great camping spot. Then it started to rain. Oh my god, it seemed like it would never stop. We were soaked. Somewhere along the line, I lost my shoes. Twelve of us jammed into our tent, and then several people began throwing up from too much pot or too much acid—inside the tent.

The entire venue turned into a mud fest. You could hardly walk anywhere without slipping or sliding. We wanted to leave, but we couldn't find our way to the portable potties, let alone find our car. The crowds were enormous, and yet, amid the chaos, it was calm, peaceful, and almost joyful.

Getting around was the most difficult part, especially without shoes. People took off their clothes and went to a waterhole to clean up. The town was unprepared for crowds and traffic. The only way we heard anything was word of mouth, or random announcements from the stage. No one was equipped or ready to deal with the mess. I remember wondering what my parents were thinking (They panicked when they saw the news). But the music was incredible and both the music and dancing proceeded non-stop, from the time we arrived until the very end. What a time!

What I remember more than the event itself is what happened a few weeks later. Life Magazine published a special issue. I drove to a store and bought it, and sat in my car, leafing through the pages when I saw a large photograph of myself—a quarter page. Someone had captured me standing, with my eyes closed, my flowing curly hair strewn with flowers, wearing a beaded necklace and a crochet vest. I wasn't aware I was being photographed; I was busy having the time of my life.

Fast forward twenty years . . . I was living in Harrison, New York, married with two young daughters, running the Christian Dior U.S. women's scarf business. Life Magazine was preparing a Woodstock retrospective and seeking people who had been there for a "Where are they now?" article. I answered the ad in The New York Times, and they selected me. My youthful picture juxtaposed to my photograph twenty years later illustrated how far I had traveled from a footloose young woman to a married businesswoman living in a suburb with two daughters.

I had always known that I wanted a career and a family, but I never imagined I would end up living so close to where I grew up. I spent most of my life between thinking as a radical and trying to "fit into" mainstream America. I never considered myself a "straight girl," more a frustrated liberal needing to mold to a "straight world." I spent almost thirty years commuting into the Big Apple, working, and helping raise two daughters. My dreams of husband, family and successful career have been fulfilled. Every once in a while I wonder what would have come of my life if I had "gone to the other side," been more radical and defiant? And everything has changed—monumentally. But in this era of YouTube, Internet dating, text messaging, and cell phones, is life better? Who knows?

Now, living in Utah, leading a much more relaxed life, I often think about that crazy, unforgettable, summer weekend, spent dancing and cavorting with a half-million strangers. It seems clear that throwing out all the "rules" in my life for one weekend had everything to do with my ability to truly relish the freedom, enjoy the music, and celebrate the underlying desire for peace that bound us together.

Pam Crowe-Weisberg earned an MA in museum studies in 2000, and in 2003 became a certified Bikram yoga instructor. Until this past spring, she was the executive director of the Kimball Art Center in Park City, Utah. She doesn't know if it stems from losing her shoes at Woodstock, but she admits to having a teensy shoe fetish ever since.

The Fences are Down

By Edward D. Christensen

In the late 1960's young men were rightfully worried about being drafted and shipped off to Vietnam. I wasn't worried. My draft card read "4A, veteran." I'd joined the navy in 1964, aged seventeen, believing media accounts of enemy gunboats attacking our ships in the Gulf of Tonkin. I served out my enlistment unaware that the entire story had been a hoax designed to increase troop levels. Still, I was one of the lucky ones. My time in the Navy amounted to a get out of jail free card from the draft. Plus, I got to go to college on the G. I. Bill.

Being in the military gives a young man a certain mindset. My ship docked in New York City in the spring of 1967. Before the crew went on liberty in the city, our officers told us we could ignore any "peaceniks and hippies" who attempted to harass us, because they weren't "men" like us. Once in college, however, I experienced a different point of view and soon let my hair grow and attended peace rallies, all while feeling a certain sense of detachment. After all, the draft couldn't get me. But of course I felt badly for anyone whose life was disrupted, or worse, as a result of Vietnam. My attitudes sound contradictory to me now, but those were contradictory times, and I was still a young man.

In 1969, my friend Frank and I were working second shift in a machine shop. About half the other guys in the shop were older World War II vets who considered us hippies. I wore bell-bottom jeans, never mind that they were uniform issue from my Navy days. When ads on the radio announced an Aquarian exposition to be held somewhere in upstate New York, Frank and I wanted to go, but my girlfriend, Lori, wanted to go too, and my tiny MG had only two seats. Luckily, my father was out of the country on business, and he had a big ol' Ford Galaxie. Frank and I quit the machine shop, and Lori quit her job at a bakery. We had to wait until Friday afternoon to get our last paycheck. When we left that night, it was already raining.

We reached our exit only to find road flares and barricades. Policemen in yellow rain slickers told us to go home, the roads were closed. We proceeded until we found an exit that wasn't blocked, and drove along back roads. It rained so hard the wipers couldn't keep up, and those back roads were blanketed in total darkness. It didn't matter. Our internal compasses were all pointing towards Woodstock. Around midnight exhaustion set in so I pulled off the road, and we slept in the car.

Saturday morning revealed that I had parked on a grassy strip beside a cornfield. I remember seeing a 1950s vintage ambulance converted to a hippie mobile, and an enormously fat local cop riding a Honda moped—so Mayberry! When two hippies dressed in ragged remnants of military uniforms drove by in a Cadillac convertible, I said, "The army and the navy are here."

We joined the migration, dozens of us, then hundreds, and by the time we were close to Yasgur's farm, thousands. Local citizens sat on their porches, watching this strange parade. All these years later, I remember a farmer in an old red pickup, milk cans of well water in the back, giving drinks to thirsty strangers, and handing out wax-paper-wrapped sandwiches to anyone who wanted one. I remember the feeling that was growing in me: that this was not just a concert; this was something more. Something important. And then word came back through the crowd, "the fences are down!" Not just the fences around a concert area, but all sorts of fences between people began coming down.

Yeah, it rained, and yeah, it was muddy. Still, people were nice to one another, like you will notice sometimes when there's a snowstorm or catastrophe—everyone helped everyone else. Half a million strangers recognized each other as brothers and sisters.

So many sights and sounds: the concert area at night, looking like the inside of a flying saucer with all the candles and lighters; the Santa-looking dude, complete with two pretty girl elves, who charged a "toll"—take a toke to pass—on the path up in the woods; the hole in the clouds that kept opening up right over us; and Jimi Hendrix at dawn on Monday. But what I remember most about Woodstock was the love. That sounds so foreign to us now, so foreign to a polarized nation. We act like it's never been that way in America, but it has. At Woodstock, we all proved that it's possible to come together, to take care of one another, and yes, to love each other. That's what I took away from Woodstock, and what still matters the most to me now. We can love one another. We've done it before.

Edward Christensen married Lori the year after Woodstock, and they are still happily married. He retired from the post office after "too many" years, and writes, reads, and travels for enjoyment. Even though he's old now, he still thinks of himself as a hippie.

Skipping the Light Fandango

By Bob Dickey

It was dead, probably around noon. Hippie record buyers were not early risers. I saw an ad in Rolling Stone and read the list aloud to Kurt.

"It's a rip-off, no way all those bands are playing one festival," replied skeptical Kurt.

"But what if . . . " I argued, "wouldn't it be cool. Hell, even if only half show up, it'll be fuckin' amazing."

We kicked the idea around, but actually going remained a pipe dream. We were students running a Milwaukee record store. However, when a friend said this guy Peter was heading east and wanted riders to split the cost of gas, the pieces fell into place. We met Peter and soon agreed to drive to suburban New York City with him, and figure it out from there.

During the drive, Peter revealed that he was a leader in the local Students for a Democratic Society and involved in every imaginable so-called radical activity at the time from anti-war to civil rights to unionizing graduate assistants. Peter not only questioned authority, he put a brick in its face. We were driving Peter's father's 1964 Jaguar Mark II, which Peter's father had left behind earlier that summer. The irony of an SDS organizer tooling around in a Jaguar was not lost on us.

When we arrived at Peter's house on Long Island Sound, his sister and her friends were packing up a VW microbus. They were festival-bound any minute. Peter made his decision, and he, Jim, Kurt, and I joined the VW crew.

The drive was uneventful until traffic crawled to a halt. Frustrated drivers first took over the opposite lane, then the shoulders. Quickly it became a four-lane one-way road. When we had not moved for thirty minutes, it suddenly set in. This is the parking lot. The trip is over. Welcome to Woodstock.

We had planned to get a motel room, which turned out to be a total pipe dream. We had no gear, just knapsacks, minimal clothes, and basic toiletries. Peter had a sleeping bag and there was an extra in the VW. So we became four guys sharing two sleeping bags, and no food despite a fair amount of cash. On Thursday, tens of thousands of people arrived. Our first thought: get tickets. When we spotted cyclone fencing lying on the ground near the planned main entrance, it was clear this had already been proclaimed a free concert.

Next: a place to sleep. We walked up the access road that ran behind the stage, split up, and began scouting around. We had landed in a colossally hairy mess of humanity. Everything was catch as catch can. That night, we slept in a field, the two sleeping bags spread across the four of us; an acceptable situation until rain started sometime after midnight. None of us awoke cheery.

Friday, Peter and I walked into Bethel. An even greater swarm was now arriving. As we walked in the opposite direction, we answered questions, estimated distances left to walk, and assured weary souls their trek was worth it. A line of people waited outside Bethel's grocery store. They would only let two in at a time, so an hour later we entered a nearly naked store. Luckily, we scored bread, peanut butter, mint jelly, chips, instant coffee, and a case of beer.

Our campsite now became several tattered grocery sacks and two soggy sleeping bags. Friday afternoon, Kurt and I sat on the still grassy hillside listening to Richie Havens, Ravi Shankar, and Incredible String Band. As dusk turned to darkness, rain clouds appeared, so we hotfooted back to move camp a hundred yards farther, near a barn. When the rains became a deluge, we "liberated" the barn.

We realized we were trespassing, but a newer steel barn stood nearby, and our barn was obviously relegated to storage. The farmhouse residents came out, looked around, and went back inside. Still, we played it cautiously, guarding our comings and goings, at least at first. Soon, others figured out that we had taken up residence in the barn and tried to join us, but we resisted, with one exception: a youngster from New York City who first claimed to be sixteen, later admitted to being thirteen. But that, too, was a lie. He was a boy with a great gift for gab, and he could roll a one-handed joint with the skill of a pot veteran. He slept inside with us.

In time we grew brazen. Jim and Peter assembled the disconnected parts of a potbelly stove and hooked it up to a working chimney. We gathered scrap wood and lit a fire, and then strung laundry lines and hung up our sleeping bags to dry. We heated water for coffee and ate canned beans. In the chaos Woodstock became, we had won the dream home lottery: dry, warm, and 500 yards from the stage.

Eventually, an old farmer in overalls walked in, saw the barn-turned-dormitory, and started yelling, "Get out of here, get out of my barn, get out now!" We moved back outside, but hung around, waiting for him to cool down, or leave.

Soon the man's son arrived. Surprisingly understanding, he said, "My dad's scared crazy you'll burn the barn down." He also told us everyone was trapped: "No one can get in or get out . . . we'll all have to make do." We struck a bargain: no fires and no smoking inside. And he agreed.

Once we had permission, we found paint-blistered Adirondack chairs and discarded tables in the loft and set up housekeeping. In the afternoons, we swung open the big barn door, pulled our chairs out, sat back, listened to the best bands in the world, and watched Woodstock Nation walk on by.

The rain became relentless, so eventually others were invited in to sleep. Monday morning when the crowd cried out "more" for the last time, we put everything back the way it had been and joined the exodus. What was left was a disaster zone, for miles, in every direction. Sleeping bags, tents, jeans, coolers, shoes, hats, jackets, tarps, garbage—the casualties of rain, mud, and druggy mayhem—all discarded, everywhere. Since we never reconnected with Peter's sister and the VW microbus, we hitched our way back to Peter's house in New Rochelle, where we took the longest, greatest, most appreciated showers in the history of personal hygiene.

Bob Dickey is a journalist and educator. Peter, Kurt, and Jim are practicing attorneys.

The Road that was Taken

By Barbara Greenough Acker

I had pulled the wrong plug and disconnected yet another international call on the PBX phone system, so naturally my boss rushed out of his office, hurling insults at me. As he walked back toward his office, he muttered, "And do something about that hair—get a wig."

A wig? He wanted me to abolish my long blond curls, curls I proudly considered my "freak flag," the one clear sign that I was an individualist, a free-thinker—and to his chagrin—a hippie in the making.

As I sat watching the red and green lights flash on the switchboard, the green ones urged, "Go, go, go!" With a clear head and a sense of purpose, I quietly unplugged all of the wires from the switchboard, stood up, and walked out of the New Jersey chemical plastics company where I had been employed since dropping out of college.

All of my friends had been talking about the Woodstock Music & Art Fair that would take place in upstate New York that weekend, and now, thanks to my square boss's chauvinist attitude, I was free to go. I called my friend Tom to hitch a ride and was surprised to find out that nobody we knew was actually going. However, Tom knew two guys who were driving up, but said they were leaving pronto. Two hours later they showed up in their shiny red Firebird, and after stuffing my sleeping bag and backpack into the trunk and hopping in, I quickly realized these guys were wasted. They chalked it up to an "early start" and agreed to let me drive so they could enjoy their "trip." We were leaving a day early, but that was fine with me.

By the time we got close to the actual site, cars clogged the rural roads, and people were abandoning their cars on the side of the road and striking off on foot. I pulled the Firebird over, grabbed my gear, and waved farewell to the two guys, who remained sitting in the back seat, grooving on something. I didn't know how far I had to walk, but simply followed the crowd. The mood was peaceful, friendly, and anticipatory. Everyone was chatting, exchanging greetings, the names of their favorite bands—and joints. The state troopers directing traffic weren't exactly friendly, but they remained calm, and simply looked the other way when someone lit up. Unlike the atmosphere almost everywhere else in America at the time, no one shouted for us "damn hippies" to cut our hair or get a job. Locals stared from their front porches, but I never heard a single unkind word. I began to feel like I was part of a nation—a nation that was going to forget, at least for a few days, about Vietnam body counts, racial discrimination, uptight employers, and controlling parents. This hippie nation's only aspiration that weekend was to sit in the sun, listen to great music, and love one another.

When we arrived at the site, I walked through the fence opening where one would expect ticket takers, but found none, dropped my gear in an open field, and gazed at the stage being set up. For the next few hours, I felt like I was watching a city grow: The stage crew was shouting orders; scaffolds were erected; and sound systems were being checked repeatedly. Row upon row of portable toilets crested the hill, while food concession stands waited for the arrival of their supplies. A shiver ran though me like electricity—this was really going to be big!

I woke up the next morning when a helicopter roared overhead and landed a few hundred feet away. I was still rubbing my eyes when Grace Slick emerged and slipped into a limousine waiting nearby on the dirt road.

Soon thereafter, young people began arriving in a steady stream, and a band of genuine hippies from Wavy Gravy's famous Hog Farm commune began organizing what they termed "a very friendly internal security." Their chief duties were monitoring bad acid trips and subduing bad behavior, while offering loving advice to the lost and confused. I volunteered to work in one of their tents, feeding organic oatmeal to children (or anyone else who wandered in) and gently talking down teenagers who were experiencing bad acid trips. I stayed there for hours—until I heard the first few notes of music coming from the stage.

Rushing back to the hill, I stopped in amazement when I reached the crown—an oceanic wave of people now covered every speck of the hill and beyond. The music floated out over the crowd, its effect more powerful than any drug I could imagine. I don't know how long I sat there listening to group after group; I don't know when the rain started, or when everyone started chanting "no rain, no rain." I do remember the feeling, the vibe, as we called it, of perfect peace and happiness. I held hands with a young GI, swaying to the music, feeling in sync even though I opposed the war he had vowed to fight. It didn't matter. We were all living in the moment, lifting our shining faces (albeit mostly from the rain) up to the music that promised us unity, music that gave us power and hope to go forward and change the world.

Four days later, ankle-deep in mud, dragging my mud-covered, soaking wet sleeping bag behind me, I headed toward the same road I had come in on. Others were also leaving, in small groups or alone, all equally tired, hungry, and silently trudging through the mud, hopefully to find their cars. We could all hear the distinct guitar chords of Jimi Hendrix's version of The Star Spangled Banner piercing the air. It seemed a fitting end for a half million people who had been brought together by music— and the idea that we really could change the world just by loving each other and opting for peace instead of violence or war.

Barbara Acker is a freelance writer and reporter whose wanderlust and search for peace brought her to countries all over the world, much to her parents' dismay. She finally settled down and raised three children. She recently moved to Denver, where she writes, bikes, and hikes with her husband, Gary.

Nice Jewish Camp Goes to Folk Festival
By D. Dina Friedman

The story of how I ended up at the Woodstock festival at the tender age of twelve is a story I've told proudly over the years. I was at sleep-away camp, and the administration decided it might be a nice thing for the "tweens" to go on a field trip to a nearby folk festival. I remember traffic, and heat, and tiny tents, which were no more than a sheet of plastic over a couple of poles. Our entire bunk had to sleep in one of those tents; the boys' bunk was in a separate tent just a few feet away. We were so hot that some of the girls decided to take off their shorts and T-shirts and parade around in their bras and underwear. When the boys hooted and ogled, the girls turned on their snotty know-it-all voices and said, "It's just like a bathing suit."

We didn't get this idea from watching mud baths and people dancing naked; we were camped on the outskirts of the farm, separate from the main action. But perhaps we caught something in spirit, the idea of not conforming to conventions—astonishing for a group of middle-class, mostly Jewish, twelve-year-old girls. We savored our few moments of rebellion before the counselors insisted we had to put our clothes back on before we could go hear the music.

By the time we got to the concert area, we were way, way far from the stage. I remember strains of Joan Baez, and Richie Havens, but mostly I remember countless people squeezed in together. Being from New York City, that didn't faze me. While drugs were not part of my consciousness, my memories of that night seem drugged and dreamlike. When I saw the movie several years later, in my twenties, and when I returned to the Woodstock museum at Yasgur's farm in my forties, nothing looked familiar, and I found myself wondering, "Had I really been there? Did this really happen?"

But I was there. And even though I was too young to be a hippie, I had already worn black armbands and sung Phil Ochs songs—with passion. What I didn't have was the counterculture consciousness. My actions were all in the realm of "good-girl." I wasn't one of the girls who took off her clothes in the tent, though it wasn't because I didn't believe I had the right to call my underwear a bathing suit . . . it was because I was too flat-chested to need a bra.

And I didn't learn about counterculture at Woodstock. In fact, before we could learn anything, the counselors woke us up early the next morning and told us we had to leave. They mentioned overcrowded conditions and a growing lack of safety. It was horribly hot anyway, and we were happy enough to sing Draft Dodger Rag on the air-conditioned bus ride home.

By the time I got to college in the mid-seventies, the Vietnam War was over, and the hippie movement had begun to fade in intensity. Yet many of those of us who came of age just a few years after the events of the sixties looked to the hippies as forbearers of the current social change movement, and to events like Woodstock as part of a vision of what was possible. I spent my late teens and early twenties wearing tie-dye, letting my hair frizz, and proudly telling my Woodstock story, as I became more active working against nuclear power and for disarmament, and even living in a social change community for a year. Then life took over. I stayed politically active in my spare time, but got a real job, had a family.

My daughter, now twenty, still refers to my husband (whose hair was past his shoulders when I met him) and me as "hippie wannabes," and I find it amusing how that part of me she still reveres as weirdly cool (whether it's clothing, politics, or attitude) is considered so passé. But while today's teens might laugh at re-enactments of Hair and dress as hippies only on Halloween, the music is still remembered and respected by the generations that have come afterwards. And Woodstock paved the way to question convention, allowing for the growing popularity of feminism, gay rights, and other social issues.

And Woodstock still has an aura that transcends generations. Occasionally when I ask my classes at the university where I teach to introduce themselves with one little known fact about themselves, when my turn comes, I offer my story. "I was at Woodstock," I say and watch their eyes widen. My vanity leaves me hoping they're thinking, "She can't possibly be old enough." I wasn't, at least not old enough to receive the full impact. But it didn't matter. I was there.

D. Dina Friedman (www.ddinafriedman.com) is the author of two young adult novels: Escaping into the Night recounts the story of teenagers who lived in forest communities during the Holocaust. Playing Dad's Song is about a boy who loses his father during 9/11 and heals from his grief through music.

From Chicago to Woodstock

By Peter Faur

When I left St. Louis for my sophomore year of college in Chicago, I knew I had spent my last summer under my mother's roof. My freshman year had given me a taste of freedom that made it difficult to live at home. And for my mom, it was loathsome having me—the former student body president of Lutheran High School South, the boyish kid she sent off to a Lutheran teachers college—come home in the summer of 1968 with a shaggy mop of hair, smoking Marlboros, and listening to the Doors singing heresies like "cancel my subscription to the Resurrection." My college years were a relatively short-lived walk on the wild side (not all that wild.), but how could she have known? We both knew, however, that we didn't want to relive a summer like that.

So the next summer, I moved with a couple of guys into a rundown, second-floor railroad apartment in Oak Park, Illinois. We lived across the street from the last stop of the Lake Street El; train cars screeched in both day and night.

That summer was everything a nineteen-year-old kid could want. I made $3.80 an hour (minimum wage was $1.30) working the night shift at the Mars candy bar factory in Oak Park. I assembled cardboard boxes while women in hairnets and white uniforms filled them with bags of Halloween-sized Three Musketeers bars.

I also moved back and forth between Vicki, my straight-arrow girlfriend from the nearby women's Catholic college, and Mary, the fun-loving, just-graduated senior from Oak Park-River Forest High School. Eventually Mary won out. Franco Zeffirelli's Romeo & Juliet was still playing that summer; a roommate said Mary reminded him of Olivia Hussey, the movie's Juliet. Mary dazzled me, and within a few months, she dumped me.

It turned out I was too much of a straight arrow for her. It's tough to shake that image when you're attending a Lutheran teachers' college—and when it's true. In the apartment one day, Mary announced she had started taking the pill, all but inviting me to enjoy her newly controlled state. I couldn't do it. It didn't seem right for a college man to take advantage of this girl just out of high school. I never did, but for awhile, she hung in with me, in part because I was going to Woodstock.

Nobody knew, of course, exactly what Woodstock would be. But to Mary and my friends, it was absolutely cool that I was going—and cooler still when it turned out to be, well, Woodstock.

My best friend, John Northlake, called me in June from St. Louis. He'd seen an ad in Crawdaddy for a New York music festival. Of the two of us, John was always the cultural pioneer and explorer. He introduced me to a lot of good music, from Bob Dylan and Mose Allison to The Who, Janis Joplin, and Canned Heat.

John bought tickets for us, a rarity at Woodstock. He flew to Chicago Wednesday night, August 13, and we both flew the next morning, student standby, to LaGuardia. At the time, it was the farthest I had ever traveled.

A college friend of mine put us up for the night at his parents' home on Long Island. On Friday, we took the Long Island Railroad to Manhattan and found our way to the Port Authority Bus Terminal. The bus took us right to the hillside at Yasgur's farm. John and I, carrying our sleeping bags, settled on our plot of grass, stage right and about two thirds of the way up the hill.

Food was scarce, and by that afternoon we were ready to eat almost anything. John guarded our stuff while I scoured the area. I found a Mexican food stand run by honest-to-god freaks. The order taker behind the counter was probably six or seven years older than I. When I paid him, he said: "A traveler's check? Hey, did you bring a cardigan too?" He took the check. I can still hear the laughter as I walked away balancing two taco platters.

Disgust over the Vietnam War was at a fever pitch in 1969, and for me, the highlight of Woodstock Saturday was Country Joe and the Fish channeling our opposition to the war with The Fish Cheer and I-Feel-Like-I'm-Fixin'-To-Die Rag.

The truth is, I learned more about Woodstock from the movie than I did from being there. We came for the music and stayed planted in one spot the whole time. We never saw the skinny-dipping, the arts festival, or the bad drug trips shown in the movie.

Plus, we left early. John and I had to head back to Manhattan Saturday night, so the last act we saw was Canned Heat. We hitchhiked to the bus station, getting rides on a Good Humor ice cream truck and the top of a station wagon. Once we got into Manhattan, we checked in to a flophouse in Times Square called the Woodstock Hotel.

I went on to become a reporter, an editor and eventually, a vice president of communications for a Fortune 500 company. The two main lessons I've carried from Woodstock:

Never assume anything about people by their appearance. There are plenty of people with good hearts and good minds walking around in all kinds of bodies dressed in all kinds of ways.

Music has the power to keep us young. I'm fifty-nine now, but I can't hear the opening riff from the CSN&Y version of Woodstock without feeling nineteen again.

Peter Faur (www.rightpoint.info) worked seven years in journalism before joining the public relations profession in industries as diverse as telecommunications, beer, chemicals, and mining. Somehow, he found time to earn master's degrees in journalism and business administration, jump out of an airplane, and travel to Europe and South America. He and his wife of thirty-three years, Pat, live in Phoenix and have two creative, independent-thinking grown children, Paul and Kate.

Riding the Crest of the Wave

By Richard Gladstein

I was fifteen years old in 1969, a freshman in high school, when I traveled to the Woodstock Music & Art Fair from Queens, with my girlfriend, Debbie, whom I had met at an anti-war demonstration in Rochester that spring.

I had just returned from hitchhiking across the United States with a friend. We had started out from Rochester, making a whirlwind trip to Los Angeles, and then back to New York. I continued to New York City to stay with Debbie. The Woodstock concert was one week away, and Debbie had friends who offered us a ride in their VW Beetle.

I don't remember where we got our tickets, but I still have them framed near my bedroom: three tickets at $6 per day. As we neared the concert site on Friday afternoon, traffic slowed to a stop, so Debbie and I decided to bail and walk the rest of the way. Luckily, we had few belongings with us. I still carried the canvas backpack and an old sleeping bag I had used to hitch across the country, and Debbie didn't have much more. Unfortunately, neither of us had a tent, very much food, money, or rain gear.

By the time we breached the hillside overlooking the stage, tens of thousands of people were already packed together. We put down our sleeping bags near the top of the hill, where drugs of all kinds could be purchased openly. Music was playing when we arrived, but we were so far away, and the sound system so poor by today's standards, that we couldn't hear very well. I recall hearing and feeling moved by Ritchie Havens's performance.

The first night the atmosphere was festive and civil. But when a mild drizzle turned into a deluge, like thousands of others, Debbie and I had nowhere to go for shelter. Not far away, the Hog Farm, and other groups who had come in old buses festooned with psychedelic designs, had set up camp, but if you didn't have a tent, you weren't allowed to stay there. The rain wasn't that bad at first; unfortunately, it rained the entire weekend—and the more it rained, the more the site, and the event, became a much more primal experience.

I don't remember feeling hunger, but I didn't eat much either. As the rain continued, I grew colder and began shivering. At one point, I tried to seek refuge inside a shelter, but it was too crowded. Virtually everyone was smoking or inhaling pot, which made the physical conditions more bearable but at some point, the experience became so overwhelming that Debbie and I ceased talking to each other. A group of bikers had settled in around us, two of who were obviously strung out on speed. At first we were a little intimidated, but the semi-circle of bikes gave us a "home."

My memories of that weekend are like a series of snapshots. On Saturday or Sunday, helicopters dropped plastic bags filled with flowers from the sky. I bathed nude with others in a nearby pond swelled by the rain. I recall Grace Slick of the Jefferson Airplane singing White Rabbit and thinking she looked like a goddess. I heard her clearly because many of the people had abandoned the formerly green hillside that had become a mudslide. I remember walking—or virtually sliding—down close to the stage, where I stood for a long while absorbed in the music. I recall banging soda cans together in rhythm with others and building fires on a hillside to keep warm.

Perhaps my single most moving memory, however, is of Jimi Hendrix playing The Star Spangled Banner. As the concert wound to a close on Monday morning, listening to Hendrix rocking our anthem made me feel patriotic. He captured what it was like to be young and yearning for a national identity when our nation was torn apart by war and riots. In my mind, Hendrix's interpretation bestowed it to a new generation. Shortly after Hendrix finished, the Woodstock Music & Art Fair was officially over. Debbie returned to Queens on the back of one of the speed freaks' motorcycle, and I hitched a ride home with a group of strangers, crammed into the back of a retooled hearse.

Returning to normal life as a high school sophomore required a major readjustment. By the end of high school, I felt exhausted, but somehow made it through college. Eventually, I finished law school, became religious, worked for legal services for the poor, married, had two children, and lived a fairly conventional life.

What did we accomplish at Woodstock? Being at Woodstock was like riding the crest of the enormous wave of social unrest and revolutionary fervor that had risen throughout the United States—and the world—during those tumultuous times.

Many believed that the real indication of patriotism and service to our country during that period came solely from those who supported and those who fought in the Vietnam War. Many felt that our generation did not properly honor those who fought and died in that war—and on some levels that was true. But it stemmed from our objections to the war, not a disdain for the soldiers, most of whom were drafted and forced to fight in a war they may not have supported either. But it is also true that the contributions of those who participated in the social upheaval and creativity of that time have never been sufficiently appreciated. We, too, made a contribution that reflected the best traditions and values of our nation: independence, tolerance, innovation, and liberty. May those traditions and values continue to move and guide us as we proceed in the twenty-first century.

Richard Gladstein lives a fulfilling life supported by family, friends, and community. He has worked as an environmental enforcement lawyer for the Justice Department, helping to protect public health and the environment for close to the last twenty years.

Seeking Wholeness

By Phaedra Greenwood

I'm probably the only person who traveled 3,000 miles to the Woodstock festival on a whim and never sat down to listen to a single set. I wasn't even a hippie. I was a poet, and, up until then, a medical secretary at Yale-New Haven Hospital, who had never been to a rock concert, or to a protest of any kind. I was against the Vietnam War, but no one ever marched in the streets of New Haven. Out of curiosity, my husband and I once took peyote together, during which I had a vision—something to do with universal wholeness. But when I came down, I felt lost and disconnected again—a poet without a purpose.

Shortly afterward, our marriage unraveled, and I needed a larger definition of family—one that would last a lifetime. I quit my job and drove alone in my VW Bug to Oregon to see Ken Kesey, who had participated in some of the earliest psychedelic experiments in the country—under government supervision. I had just finished reading his novel, Sometimes a Great Notion, and thought he might have valuable insights that could help me find my way. But when I arrived at Kesey's farm, he proved elusive. His band of followers, however, known widely as The Merry Pranksters, had signed up to work at a rock festival in upstate New York, for a dollar a day as part of the security Please Force, and invited me along. "No thanks," I said, and meant it. But the night before the caravan left, on an impulse, I grabbed my traveler's checks, locked my car, and hopped on the last bus.

Thirteen days later, upon arrival at Max Yasgur's farm, thousands of hippies in colorful costumes swirled around me. I sat down to sew stars on my jeans, a sign I was joining their frivolity, but inside I still felt faceless and invisible. Two skinny guys in black leather showed up with a tripod and a camera and asked me to hop on one of the empty commune buses and gaze out the window, as if arriving for the first time. That's me going solo in the opening shots of the Woodstock film, gazing at the ground, too shy to look up and enjoy my fifteen seconds of fame.

Later, around a campfire, I met a sassy fellow with glasses and a bushy mustache who had come in from the Hog Farm commune in New

Mexico. I glommed onto Stoney instantly, partly because of my "faceless in the crowd" thing, but also because his touch conveyed mojo. In a haystack, by the break of dawn, I found myself reflected in his blue-gray eyes. And suddenly, we were kissing. Kissing.

Later, after dropping some Purple Haze, Stoney and I were lying under a tree on a hill above the stage area when a sudden wind thrashed the treetops and snarling clouds with teeth and claws swept down on us like demons. As we scrambled to our feet, musicians onstage rushed to cover their equipment. And then the power died, and curtains of rain wafted over the audience.

"The chickens!" I yelped. Stoney and I had been babysitting a flock of baby chicks brought to entertain children. I sprinted up the hill to the aviary with Stoney close behind. The baby chicks were soaked and beeping in high C so we swooped them into four cardboard boxes and tromped down to the festival trailers searching for light—and heat.

There was no light, or heat. Seeing our plight, a man in a leather hat pointed to a new maroon Chrysler. "Take them in there and crank up the heat," he said, grinning.

Stoney and I, along with two helpers, crowded into the car, turned on the blower, and held up the chicks one-by-one to dry them. Soon fluffy yellow chicks bounced around like popcorn, happily pooping on the upholstery. Afraid we would smash them if we moved, we sat still, laughing. Shortly thereafter, power was re-established, and Stoney and I transported the chicks back to the aviary.

Stoney and I then left to spend the rest of the evening helping the Please Force distribute food and medical supplies. At some point, I lost track of Stoney, probably because we were all traipsing around as high as kites. Eventually I finished distributing blankets and walked out into the dark. Alone. I walked until I came upon a circle of folks standing under a light pole, humming and passing a bottle from mouth to shining mouth. I crept close enough to see their joyous faces and momentarily felt even lonelier. A circle seemed like such a belonging thing.

Suddenly the circle broke, and Stoney slid one hand around my waist. Someone passed the bottle, and I took a sip of wine. After a few more swigs, I tipped my head back the way the others did and let the breath slide from my throat in a long, resonant note that merged with the group hum: "OOOOmmmmmmmm." I continued humming until the top of my head buzzed and I felt newly blessed with a sense of wholeness, until I knew that I would never feel so sharply disconnected again. No matter where I went, or what came down, I had found kindred spirits, at long last, a family that would last forever.

Phaedra Greenwood is a freelance writer whose nature memoir, Beside the Rio Hondo, was published by Sunstone Press of Santa Fe. For five years, Phaedra worked as a journalist and columnist for The Taos News, a prize-winning weekly in Northern New Mexico. She has won many awards for her short stories, poems, and articles. Learn more about Phaedra on www.phaedragreenwood.com.

Last Minute Hookup

By Glenn Nystrup

On August 17, 1969, I was sitting with some friends on the front porch of an old farmhouse a few miles from the University of Connecticut in Storrs. I had recently rented the house with its barn and meadows, and even a horse. It would soon be filled with a brother, a cousin, and several friends, all of whom were attending UConn.

We were talking about the Woodstock festival and had been going back and forth for twenty-four hours about our chances of getting in if we were to make the long drive. We first heard that tickets were sold out; then that barriers were down and tickets were now meaningless; then that highways were closed because of traffic; and then that the third largest city in New York was forming with virtually no government. The longer we procrastinated the more it seemed obvious we had missed our moment and would stick around, hanging out on the porch, enjoying a beautiful summer day.

It all changed when Richard's older brother called, and Richard excitedly turned to me and said, "My brother is the assistant manager at the Holiday Inn near the Woodstock festival, and he can get us in. He also said that most of the performers are staying at the hotel, and we should get our butts over there right away."

We all immediately leaped into the air and began shouting "road trip!" We grabbed a few things, piled into Richard's station wagon, and headed west.

By the time we reached the hotel, it was dark. We greeted Richard's brother and sat in the lounge waiting to see if we would get to the concert. I looked to one side of the room and saw Grace Slick and Jack Cassidy. At a table in the corner were members of The Who, and minutes later, Janis Joplin walked by.

By the time we finished our first drink, we heard a commotion going on. We were informed that Buffy Sainte-Marie had just organized a car caravan to travel to the concert site several miles away. We hopped aboard and were soon on our way, desperately hoping our car would not run out of gas. If we were to stop for gas now, we would lose the escort.

And so we drove deep into the heart of what seemed to be a living creature—hundreds of thousands of unified, undulating bodies—and stopped within a few yards of the stage. The police escort had taken us all of the way in. I had a sense of something massive, even though we could only see part of it because of darkness and the sheer size of it all.

We knew that the Jefferson Airplane—one of our favorite bands—was scheduled to play that evening. We also knew we hadn't missed them, since they were at the hotel when we were there. While other bands played, we took turns with the two stage area passes we were given by Richard's brother, getting good views. Without the passes I recall that the views were difficult, though the music was great.

As light began to seep into the sky the next morning, Jefferson Airplane still had not played. We watched as the light expanded our views of the fields of people, noticing that they looked colorful, tired, yet remarkably filled with energy. We were there one night without sleeping and already felt a bit worn. Our water and food were gone.

Jefferson Airplane finally took the stage, so we got to hear them up close, along with the shouting of half a million fans. We stayed for most of their show. Toward the end we packed ourselves into the car and began the drive out. A moving vehicle proved a very attractive thing, so we soon had people clinging to the car in every way possible. I don't know if the car was even visible from a distance. Only a swarm of bodies creeping along the ground could be seen. We were driving at about five miles per hour. The gas gage was resting on E, and we had not seen any gas stations close by. We hoped the extra weight would not stop us in our tracks.

As we were driving off, we got to really see the magnitude of the event. I had never seen so many people in one place, packed in, getting along, with smiles on their faces. It all seemed to be a wild free-for-all, without rules, yet with something more. Something was definitely driving the heart of what was happening; something that was shared by the many souls there; something that allowed a tremendous number of people to cram together, with less than comfortable accommodations, enjoying themselves, and primarily treating each other well. The word that kept coming to me was, well, awesome.

We did make it to a gas station, and made our way home, excitedly talking about the fact that we had gone from our front porch to navigating our black Ford station wagon through one of the most significant events of our generation.

The Woodstock festival didn't need to last forever. The communes didn't need to last forever. They had a profound effect, on those who attended and many others not directly involved. It all set a tone that still carries forward . . . and even now, forty years later, we're still telling the tales of that legendary weekend.

Glenn Nystrup and a partner run a small private day school for students with Asperger's syndrome in Hyde Park, New York. They recently escorted students on a trip to the Woodstock festival site, where they visited the Bethel Woods Center for the Arts. The students knew about Woodstock, but mostly they loved running around the site.

The Axis of Boomer Wisdom

By Dixon Hearne

We baby boomers have straddled and stretched across nearly six decades of unprecedented change, with a spoiled "me-first" genetic marker as one salient contribution to the generation we have raised "our way." We were also the best and the brightest—by SAT measures, at least—and our uproar is still reverberating in every conceivable direction. We have revolutionized lifestyle and music and dress and language in our desperation to establish some cultural legitimacy—what we tagged, "counterculture." The Beatles led us in our anthem, and, along with the Stones, pointed the way through the doo wop and daddy-o days of our childhood to a brave new age, culminating in the Great Tribal Gathering of '69—Woodstock.

I did not go. Nor did millions of others, and that was a travesty far greater than missing the prom or failing to graduate. Like many other Boomers, I had to witness Woodstock vicariously through newscasts and friends who did attend and dutifully reported the experience in every imaginable detail, reports of drug-and-alcohol induced spasms of euphoria trips to otherworldly regions beyond the grasp of earthbound thought, and all electric and self-satisfying.

Back home, we felt suddenly important by association with someone who was there to witness—our eyes and ears on the event of the century, our heralds of a great change a'comin'. And oh how they gloried in the fifteen minutes of fame we heaped upon them.

It was the "End of the Beginning" or the "Beginning of the End"—depending upon who you were then, are now, and how it continues to be reported and discussed. For those of us who believed, it truly did seem a dawning of The Age of Aquarius. We had made the final cosmic leap. We were no longer L-7 or squaresville. We were "cool" and," "far out" and "groovy." You could see it in our faces, our unisex hair, our bell-bottoms, and sandals—right up to the day that disco killed the radio, then turned another page and never looked back. The day when sandals suddenly seemed too flat, as if platform heels could make us rise again with renewed dreams and transitory pleasures and assure us that the party will never end.

But childhood did end—for those who were fortunate—and war ended too late for those who weren't. And we found ourselves thrust upon a world that still did not understand our generation or our struggle to be differently alike, while living an adult world where survival of the fittest was skewed heavily toward the opposing team. The Woodstock generation went kicking and screaming, but we survived, even thrived, and lived to realize the glorious fruits of the last children's crusade. Girls, we now know, can study and learn just as well in pants, long hair is not a stable and inextricable predictor of success (or lack thereof), rock and roll has never been unquestionably linked to cancer, and the nation's churches have not closed up shop.

We have mellowed and reflected on our past—still do—and what our legacy will have been—and we are not through yet. Into the vastness of our current information age, we can lay claim to its roots in every field, trace our lineage to the very spark that set so many things in play. By our hands and minds, we have wittingly and unwittingly hewn a technological image of our very selves, a transitory technology that makes invention itself obsolete—for every new idea is constantly in want of a replacement.

We've sped the process to a point that it seems to pass us by, advancing for the first time at a pace uncomfortable for the Eternal Generation. We find ourselves line dancing, surfing the net, ballroom dancing with the stars, competing with ourselves again, and taking note of the mindless, selfish, narcissistic generations that follow behind. We don't do communes anymore, or crash on pallets ten abreast or in cramped Volkswagens or in city parks. We do not down a fifth of Jack Daniels or chug a pitcher of Bud in sixty seconds, or otherwise drink ourselves under a table on a dare. Nor do most picket or protest in freezing rains or sweltering heat—we've passed the torch, the signs, the banners, and the microphone to our kids.

We have learned to fit in, to find our place in the bigger picture. We settle for less than all our dreams. We count our IRA dividends, eye the stock market, and thank some unknown being for the wisdom of 401Ks and social security—for we never counted on being this old someday. The cup of life may have quietly passed half-empty, but for a generation raised on eternal hopes and insistence on endless possibility and easy access, the cup will always be half-full. And in many ways, Woodstock was the very axis of wisdom for my generation—igniting international change while weaving the value of counter-cultural ideals into the vibrant tapestry of modern life. Turns out I was there, still am in a way.

Dixon Hearne teaches and writes in Southern California—with the help of his two Bichons who insist on having the last word. His stories can be found in Mature Living, Louisiana Literature, and forthcoming in Humor for the Boomer's Heart and Rocking Chair Reader: Christmas Traditions. He is the author of three short story collections.

Woodstock Glossary

Acid tests – Ken Kesey and the Merry Pranksters held parties where guests ingested LSD, sometimes without their knowledge. Kesey believed in confronting personal fears under the influence of hallucinogenic drugs and constantly pushed the limits with his own experimentations. Acid tests were also held in public places, such as musical events at Bill Graham's Fillmore West.

Atlantic City Pop Festival – Rock festival held at the Atlantic City Racetrack on August 1, 2 and 3, 1969. Many of the artists at Woodstock had previously appeared in Atlantic City.

Ken Babbs – Ken Kesey's best friend and the leader of the Merry Pranksters' Woodstock squad. Babbs and at least forty hippies piled into five school buses, one of which was the infamous Furthur (see Furthur) to attend Woodstock.

Bethel, New York – The small town in New York's Borscht Belt that hosted the 1969 Woodstock Music & Art Fair after it was ousted from Wallkill.

Counterculture – What the news media used to refer to the social revolution that swept North America, Western Europe, Japan, Australia and New Zealand during the 1960s and early 1970s.

Furthur – The most famous Merry Prankster bus immortalized by author Tom Wolfe in The Electric Kool-Aid Acid Test. It had a custom, psychedelic paint job and a Plexiglas bubble on top, and it was packed with sound gear.

Hippies - Primarily youths of the 1960s who dropped out of, or at least experimented with a break from, conventional culture. Hippies typically eschewed materialism, conformity, and the military-industrial complex (the establishment) and embraced the drug culture (particularly marijuana and LSD), psychedelic rock, and free love. Some migrated to rural areas, where they embraced eastern philosophies, communal living, and organic farming. In the late 1960s, most hippies were for civil rights and against the Vietnam War. Male hippies often grew their hair to their shoulders and longer; many female hippies favored braless tops and long, flowing skirts. Fringed leather vests, headbands, and love beads were among their favorite accessories.

Abbie Hoffman - A cofounder of the Youth International Party (Yippies), an irreverent left-wing organization. Hoffman later wrote Woodstock Nation, a book about his experiences—including being knocked off the stage by The Who's Pete Townshend. At the time of Woodstock, Hoffman was awaiting trial as part of the Chicago Seven, who were charged with disrupting the 1968 Democratic convention.

Hog Farm – A group of hippies who began as pig farmers and purchased land next to a Hopi Indian reservation in New Mexico to form a huge commune. They earned a stellar reputation for handling large hippie gatherings and drug overdoses. Woodstock Ventures hired them to handle food preparation, medical supplies, and "security" via their "Please Force."

Holiday Inn Monticello - Where the Woodstock performers stayed

I forget - Secret password of the Hog Farm Please Force security volunteers.

Jook Savages - A group of artists and musicians who participated in the
Watts acid test held by Ken Kesey and later moved to San Francisco,
where they were prominent in the hippie community.

Ken Kesey – One of the founders and leaders of the counterculture
movement. Kesey bought a farm in Oregon, with the earnings from his
two bestsellers, One Flew Over the Cuckoo's Nest (1962) and Sometimes
a Great Notion (1964), which became a haven for the Merry Pranksters.

Timothy Leary - a psychologist, an assistant college professor at UC
Berkeley, and a lecturer at Harvard, who is most famous as a free-
spirited proponent of the therapeutic and spiritual benefits of LSD (which
led to his being dismissed by Harvard). He coined and popularized the
catch phrase "Turn on, tune in, drop out."

LSD – A chemical named lysergic acid diethylamide, more popularly
known as "acid." The drug occasionally induced hallucinations. Negative
experiences were called "bummers" or "bum trips."

Merry Pranksters - A group of hippies who launched the first acid tests in
San Francisco and hung out at Ken Kesey's farm in Oregon and his
ranch in La Honda, California. Their Magic Bus Trip across the United
States, in 1964, was chronicled in Tom Wolfe's 1968 book The Electric
Kool-Aid Acid Test.

Monterey Pop Festival - Held in Monterey, California, in 1967.
Monterey Pop is the 1968 concert film by D.A. Pennebaker that
documented that festival.

Owsley LSD - Owsley Stanley was the "underground chemist" who
provided massive amounts of his White Lightning LSD at very
affordable prices. Some estimated that he produced enough LSD for five

million trips, vast amounts of which he freely gave away. He was also a revolutionary sound engineer for The Grateful Dead, credited with developing their "wall of sound."

Summer of Love - 1967, the summer thousands of young hippies and aspiring hippies flocked to San Francisco's Haight-Ashbury district.

Elliott Tiber – President of the Chamber of Commerce and proprietor of the El Monaco Motel in White Lake, New York, where the organizers and some of the performers stayed. Tiber had a town permit to sponsor a (small) music festival in 1969 that allowed the organizers to switch the site from Wallkill to Bethel. He later wrote a fascinating book, Knock on Woodstock, about his extensive involvement.

Turtle Island - English language translation of many Native American tribes' terms for the continent of North America.

Michael Wadleigh – The documentary filmmaker who had filmed Martin Luther King Jr., and Bobby Kennedy and George McGovern on the campaign trail in 1968. He had begun using rock 'n roll music to highlight social and political upheaval and accepted the offer to film Woodstock, even though he had to invest $50,000 of his own money up front.

Wallkill, New York – The original site of the Woodstock Ventures' music festival. The 300-acre industrial site was retracted one month before the concert because of public protests. The town's residents worried about sex-crazed, drugged out hippies invading their town and threatened to "shoot the first hippie that walked into town," reported one member of the Woodstock Ventures' team. Publicity about what had happened reaped a bonanza of press that likely contributed to the exodus to White Lake/Bethel.

Wavy Gravy - The leader of the Hog Farm. Hugh Romney, a former beatnik comic, changed his name to Wavy Gravy. He was also known by the Hog Farm as their "minister of talk." When asked to handle food preparation and security for Woodstock, Wavy Gravy rounded up eighty-five Hog Farmers and fifteen Hopis. He donned a Smokey-the-Bear suit and armed himself with a bottle of seltzer and a rubber shovel. "We're the hippie police," Gravy announced as he and his entourage stepped off the plane on Monday, Aug. 11, 1969, at JFK airport in New York.

Fred Weintraub - The original owner and host of The Bitter End in New York City's Greenwich Village. Later, as an executive at Warner Bros., Weintraub put his job on the line by giving Woodstock Ventures $100,000 for the film. Warner Brothers was about to go out of business and the Woodstock movie saved the company, as documented in the book, Easy Riders, Raging Bulls.

White Lake – One of four lakes in Bethel, New York.

Woodstock, New York - A bohemian enclave in Ulster County that had been known as a haven for artists and writers since the turn of the century. By the mid-1960s, well-known musicians such as Bob Dylan and The Band had settled in Woodstock.

Woodstock—Three Days of Peace and Music (1970) - The film of the festival that received the Academy Award for Documentary Feature and was deemed "culturally significant" by the United States Library of Congress. In 1994, Woodstock: The Director's Cut was released, expanded to include Janis Joplin as well as additional performances by Jefferson Airplane, Jimi Hendrix, and Canned Heat, not seen in the original version of the film.

Woodstock Ventures Inc. – The quartet of men who banded together to create the festival. Their corporate name (and the festival name) arose from their desire to raise money to build a state-of-the-art recording studio in Woodstock. Contrary to myth, the festival was never intended to take place in Woodstock. The partners were Michael Lang, a manager of a rock band; Artie Kornfeld, an executive at Capitol Records; and two venture capitalists, John Roberts and Joel Rosenman.

Max Yasgur – Owner of the dairy farm in Bethel who leased the land to Woodstock Ventures for $75,000. Yasgur was the biggest milk producer in Sullivan County, with delivery routes, a massive refrigeration complex, and a pasteurization plant. The 600 acres that Ventures sought were only part of the Yasgur property, which extended along both sides of Route 17B in Bethel.

Woodstock Performers

Friday August 15, 1969

Richie Havens

Swami Satchidananda - gave the invocation for the festival

Country Joe McDonald, played a separate set from his band, The Fish

John Sebastian

Sweetwater

Bert Sommer

Tim Hardin

Ravi Shankar

Melanie

Arlo Guthrie

Joan Baez

Saturday, August 16, 1969

Quill

Keef Hartley Band

Santana

Incredible String Band

Canned Heat

Leslie West/Mountain

Ten Years After

Janis Joplin

Grateful Dead

Creedence Clearwater Revival

Sly & the Family Stone

The Who

Jefferson Airplane with Grace Slick

Sunday, August 17, 1969

Joe Cocker

Country Joe & The Fish

The Band

Blood, Sweat & Tears

Johnny Winter

Crosby, Stills, Nash & Young

Neil Young

Paul Butterfield Blues Band

Sha-Na-Na

Jimi Hendrix

Famous no-shows that most people assume were there: The Rolling Stones opted out. Bob Dylan was invited but never committed to attend. Joanie Mitchell had a traumatic experience at the Atlantic City Festival two weeks prior and did not attend Woodstock. Later, she wrote the song that became its legendary theme: Woodstock.

Woodstock Stats

Cost for tickets for the three-day 1969 festival: $18

Cost for tickets for the 30th anniversary festival: $150

Distance between Woodstock (the town) and Bethel: 48 miles

Mileage from New York City to Bethel: 98 miles

Average drive time from New York City that weekend: 8 hours

Population of Bethel in 1969: 3,900

Traffic backup: 20 miles

Deaths: 2 (one heroin overdose; one run over by a tractor)

Births: 2 (one in traffic jam, one airlifted out)

Reported violent crimes or burglary: 0

Days required to clean site: 5

Cost of cleanup: $100,000

Original festival budget: $500,000

Final cost: $2.4 million

Tickets pre-sold:186,000*

Crowd estimates: State Police, 450,000; Bethel historian, 700,000 (he said the aerial photos used by the police to estimate the size did not include those in tents and under trees.)

Number of people who never made it to the site: 250,000

Amount spent on talent: $180,000

Highest paid performer: Headliner Jimi Hendrix $32,000 (The Who received around $12,000, twice their usual fee; others in same range or lower)

Amount Hendrix requested: $150,000 (which he had recently been paid for another performance)

Number of months between Jimi Hendrix's performance and his death:13

Number of months between Janis Joplin's performance and her death:14

Number of New York City policemen moonlighting: less than 10 (at $90 a day)

Cost of one ounce of marijuana: $15

Estimated percentage of festival attendees smoking marijuana: 90

Length of Richie Havens's performance: 3 hours (stalling until other musicians could be flown in)

Number of portable toilets: 600

Pounds of canned food, sandwiches, and fruit flown in by emergency helicopters: 1,300

Number of sandwiches prepared by the Women's Group of the Jewish Community Center of Monticello and distributed by the Sisters of the Convent of St. Thomas: 30,000

Frankfurters and hamburgers consumed on the first day: 500,000

Amount of rainfall on Friday night: 5 inches

Number of medical cases: 5,162 (drug reactions, cut feet, and sun blindness)

Number of miscarriages: 8

Number of drug charges: 177

Average fine: $25

Number of tickets refunded:12,000-18,000

Worldwide box office gross (in dollars) made by 1979 on Woodstock movie: $50,000,000

*Ticket sales were limited to record stores in the greater New York City area, or by mail via a post office box at the Radio City Station post office in Midtown Manhattan.

*Mostly derived from www.woodstock69.com, and additional resources. The website doesn't reveal its sources, but they spent years amassing "fun facts" and memorabilia so they're probably well within the ballpark. See their website for a whole lot more fun facts.

Timeline of Music and Social Unrest:

1967

Paul McCartney told Life Magazine he had taken LSD and it brought him closer to God.

The Beatles transmitted All You Need is Love from their Abbey Road Studio in London to 400-million people via the first global satellite/television linkup.

When The Daughters of American Revolution barred Joan Baez from performing in Boston's Constitution Hall because of her "anti-nationalist statements" against the Vietnam War, Baez performed a free concert outdoors for 30,000 cheering fans.   1967

Race riots plague cities.

Thousands flock to San Francisco for infamous "Summer of Love"

Anti-war protesters march on Pentagon in Washington, D. C.

474,000 troops in Vietnam (13,000 dead)

1968

Hair, chronicling the counterculture Hippies, became the first Broadway musical to feature frontal nudity and achieved instant success.

The First Edition of Rolling Stone magazine hit American newsstands. Each magazine had a roach clip attached as a freebie. John Lennon was on the cover.

At no time in American history has youth possessed the strength it possesses now. Trained by the music and linked by the music, it has the power for good to change the world. Ralph J. Gleason, Rolling Stone

Amid the violence and fear of further violence, some radio stations banned The Rolling Stone's Street Fighting Man 1968

Tet Offensive threatens Saigon and 100 cities in South Vietnam

Martin Luther King is assassinated; over 65,000 armed guards quell race riots in over 100 U. S. cities.

Students for a Democratic Society take over buildings on Columbia campus.

Robert Kennedy is assassinated after winning California primary.

Democratic Convention in Chicago is site of bloody riots in which police attack protestors.

Richard Nixon wins presidential election.

1969

Over 450,000 people flock to a small New York hamlet for 3 days of Peace & Music, creating the most famous rock concert of all time – Woodstock.   1969

Neil Armstrong and Nelson Aldrin are first men to walk on the moon.

Massive anti-war demonstrations occur in Washington, D. C.

Student deferments eliminated and draft lottery begins.

President Nixon orders bombing of Cambodia.

1970

The Beatles disband.

Nixon orders "incursion" into Cambodia.

National Guard kills 4 Kent State students during protests over Cambodia action.

448 universities and colleges close in protest of Cambodia action and Kent State murders.

About the Author

Susan Reynolds began her professional career as a journalist and, since 2008, has authored, edited, or coauthored more than 50 nonfiction and fiction books. Her nonfiction works include Everything Enneagram, Everything Personal Finance for Single Mothers, Train Your Brain to Get Rich, and Fire Up Your Writing Brain.

The idea for Woodstock Revisited arose after Susan spent a year in Paris (writing of course) and often found young Europeans fascinated by the mere fact that she had gone to Woodstock. She remains passionate about music, her country, and peaceful insurrection when vital freedoms and principles are at stake. She's proud that this anthology captures a piece of Woodstock's legacy for her children, her nieces and nephews, and hundreds of thousands of other people's children.

Learn more about Susan on www.fireupyourwritingbrain or on her Amazon Author Page

https://www.amazon.com/SusanReynolds/e/B001K8AM40?ref=sr_ntt_srch_lnk _1&qid=1562494040&sr=1-1

(She's not the Susan Reynolds who writes Medieval history books; she's the other one! Look for Woodstock Revisited on her list of books.)

Printed in Great Britain
by Amazon